D1458547

The Binds That Tie

The Binds That Tie

Overcoming Standoffs and Stalemates in Love Relationships

by

RICHARD DRISCOLL

Lexington Books

D.C. Heath and Company · Lexington, Massachusetts · Toronto

Library of Congress Cataloging-in-Publication Data

Driscoll, Richard.
The binds that tie : overcoming standoffs and stalemates in love relationships / by Richard Driscoll.
p. cm.
ISBN 0-669-24419-8 (alk. paper)
1. Marriage. 2. Communication in marriage. 3. Interpersonal relations. I. Title.
HQ734.D76 1990
646.7'8—dc20 90-35895
CIP

Published simultaneously in Canada
Printed in the United States of America
International Standard Book Number: 0-669-24419-8
Library of Congress Catalog Card Number: 90-35895

The paper used in this publication meets the minimum requirements of American National Standard for Information Sciences—Permanence of Paper for Printed Library Materials, ANSI Z39.48-1984.

∞™

Year and number of this printing:

91 92 93 94 95 8 7 6 5 4 3 2 1

To

KEITH DAVIS

and

PETER OSSORIO

who introduced me to the commonsense
wonders of ordinary language psychology,

and to

NANCY DAVIS

my colleague and wife,
who journeys with me while
I learn so much the hard way.

Contents

PART IV
The Mix and Mismatch of Sexual Interests

List of Figures

Preface

By the time couples seek my assistance, they are near the ends of their tethers and running low on patience. In some fifteen years as a marriage and family therapist, I have listened as husbands and wives tell me about their own hurts and complaints and about the anger and boredom they feel with those they chose years ago as their lifelong partners. I hear about how they have a right to expect more from a marriage, and how their partners have failed to provide even the bare minimum of understanding and consideration, and good sex.

I concluded long ago that the tale first told is not an unfinished story, with the conclusion hanging between the hands of a talented therapist and the whims of fate. The tale first told is only the unhappy conclusion, for what is missing is the beginning and the middle of the story along with sufficient information to figure out how the marriage got so far off course. Quarreling mates provide many arguments but only the bare sketches of the full story, and usually from their own sides of the standoff.

As a marriage therapist, it is my job to make inquiries, gather information, assemble the pieces, then ghost-write for couples a credible story of their marriages. The tales that emerge are much richer than the commonplace complaints and justifications and are infinitely more fascinating. Only when the words and actions of one mate are compared and fit into place with those of the other do the inner workings of a marriage become truly visible.

Whether couples seek counseling in the storm of an infidelity or the simple boredom of unmet expectations, there are always typical routines and communication patterns that have led up to their current exasperation. Often blending into the background, such routines are nonetheless the identifying features of unfulfilling marriages, holding husbands and wives together in unsatisfying interactions neither can rise above. As a marriage therapist, it is my job to identify these patterns, to show how they work, and to help couples free themselves from them to find greater joy and vitality in their lives together.

In this book I present the inner workings of various troublesome patterns, along with plans to escape from them, in the hope that I may guide couples through difficult hours on the journey to a new and freer life in commited relationships.

Acknowledgments

THIS book was some four years in preparation. Many thanks to Keith Davis, for his intellectual support over the years; to Rita, who convinced me time was on my side; and to Christopher, Jonathan, and Kari, for not minding too much when I was only half there.

Thanks to Becky, Lloyd, John, Doug, Ellis, and Ginny, who helped straighten out snafus and liven up my characters; to Nancy, for critical editing available on short notice; and to Sherrie, for corralling stray words and for loving my writing.

Thanks to my dinosaur word processor, which served as typist and tried not to break down at critical times any more than was absolutely necessary; and to the small grant from the Nancy Davis foundation, which helps support our family while I write.

Thanks also to my many clients who volunteered their marriages to field test my material.

The Binds That Tie

Part I

Patterns in Marriages

Patterns are the trademarks of human relationships, as we continue in familiar routines over the years. The inclinations of one partner weave together with those of the other partner, forming the patterns of lives spent together in intimate relationships.

Some of our patterns are productive and satisfying, while others are troublesome or personally harmful. Those that are beneficial need no special explanation, aside from ordinary common sense. We consider them right, or good, or proper, or fun, or at least safe or convenient. We continue in them because they are comfortable and satisfying, and because they seem better than the available alternatives. When something works, why change it?

It is those patterns that are tiresome and unwanted that require special explanation. Why do we continue in routines that are harmful to us? And perhaps more importantly, once in these routines, how do we break free of them? The inner workings of harmful patterns, and the ways we ourselves unwittingly participate in them, are of utmost importance to all of us. By understanding our patterns, we gain the power to reshape and revitalize our most important relationships.

Patterns are too easily overlooked, not because they are unfamiliar or obscure but precisely because they are so obvious. Like the air we breathe or the way we shake hands, patterns are so commonplace that they are simply taken for granted. Yet the more we look for them, the more we see of them. And as we look in on them, we renew an acquaintance with what have been our old and close companions all along.

1

It's Obvious (Once You See It)

TROUBLESOME patterns can sap the vitality from an otherwise strong relationship. Couples often feel upset, irritated, resigned, or simply bored by their familiar routines, as they replay and restage and then replay again the same unsatisfying scenes from a marriage.

Perhaps you and your mate quarrel—which is normal, of course. But you seem to have the *same* quarrels over and over. Your arguments begin in the ordinary ways: you bite into the old worn-out subjects, continue along familiar lines, wear each other down, then finish without resolution. Three days later, you repeat the squabble again, and run its full course.

Perhaps you are upset by some of the ways your mate acts, as many are, but find yourself helpless when your requests for change remain unheard and unheeded. Small irritations accumulate and grow, until you get so caught up in the aggravations that you too become part of the problem. These are some of the indications of unpleasant patterns in marriages.

Troublesome patterns seem to carry us along against our better judgment and in spite of our apparent wishes for change. Various accounts for why we continue in these patterns have been proposed.

Some argue that we are irrational, and that we unconsciously but willfully cause our own misfortunes.[1] Although we all know people who indulge themselves in more than their share of misery, I have always been skeptical of the argument that people love to suffer. The phrase "love to suffer" seems like an oxymoron, like "jumbo shrimp" or "idiot savant." Where is the joy in suffering?

Those who choose to suffer do so as a means to further aims,[2] so it is important to understand their real purposes. Some suffer as a way to get attention and obligate friends (saying, by their sour moods, "It's your job to cheer me up!"). Some suffer to avoid criticism ("You cannot kick a dog when he's whining at your feet!"). Some suffer as penance, to affirm their moral character ("I am a good person because I am willing to suffer for my wrongs!"); or even to send an angry message ("Look how miserable you have made me feel about myself, you rat!"). For some, subordination and pain is a condition for sexual arousal, by absolving the masochist of responsibility ("I can't help myself—she's forcing me to do it!"). But even the most miserable individuals want more out of life than unhappiness.

Some argue that unwanted patterns persist because we are the mere products of our conditioning—prisoners of our maladaptive pasts. But while we come from our pasts, we are surely more than the automatic continuations of old routines. We are also active participants in our lives—choosing our lines and choreographing our steps to fit with those of the characters who play opposite us.

Perhaps the trouble is that we give ourselves too many negative messages, as the advocates of positive thinking contend. Should we strive to replace negative beliefs with more positive ones about ourselves? Surely an "I can" message to oneself is almost always better than an "I cannot" message. Convince yourself you can do something, and you are on your way. But many of us are wary of false reassurance, and find it hard to convince ourselves that a relationship that is clearly going wrong will work out. There is more to a good marriage than convincing oneself that it can be good.

Patterns Are Self-Perpetuating. Troublesome patterns seem to follow an inner logic of their own, which causes them to continue in spite of our wishes to change. Husbands and wives often act in such a way that they unwittingly contribute to the very problems that they are trying to resolve. Neither partner wants troublesome patterns to continue, and each is trying to get something he or she wants out of the marriage. Yet by their attempts to improve their marriages, they inadvertently perpetuate their unwanted routines.[3] The actions of one partner unintentionally contribute to the unwanted actions of the other, which contribute further to the actions of the first, and so on in a self-perpetuating fashion. Ironically, they are trapped by their own good intentions.

The self-perpetuating loop provides a sound explanation for a broad range of otherwise perplexing psychological problems. Suppose you are walking a dog, and he winds his leash around a telephone pole. Wanting to get away from the pole, it makes perfect sense from his perspective to continue going forward. Yet so long as he goes forward, he only gets himself wound more tightly. Ironically, he is caught by his own attempt to get loose. To free himself, he has to reverse his course, and go backward.

Going full speed ahead makes sense from the limited perspective of the one caught up in a self-perpetuating pattern. In pattern after pattern, each action in the sequence is seen to have rhyme and reason to the one who takes it. The inner logic of the patterns confirms our rationality, in spite of our problems. A closer look shows the reasonable aims of our actions, as well as the ways in which the actions backfire.

Personal problems continue not because we are mindless or weak, but because our perspectives are too limited and our strengths misdirected. We are not irrational, but merely shortsighted. Too focused on the immediate moment, we miss the larger picture. Too concerned with the next step, we do not look up to see what is beyond the next bend when the path turns and heads back to where we have already been.

Look now at a common self-perpetuating pattern in a marriage.

Workaholic Provider—Dissatisfied Partner

Some promises seem to be made to be broken. It is after eight o'clock when William finally arrives home. He has worked into the evenings, and on Saturdays as well, for almost as many years as he and Diane have been married. But tonight is their anniversary, and Diane is ill-prepared for more of the same. She had not really expected him around six o'clock, as he had promised. Allowing for the usual unexpected delays, she figured he would be home around seven. The babysitter has been there for an hour, playing with the children, while Diane waits in silence. When William finally arrives, she is so hurt and angry she could take a swing at him.

"But you promised!" she accuses. "Just this once we were going to have the whole evening together. I cannot understand how you always do this to me!" Tears beginning, she turns away from him and heads for the bedroom.

William is uncomfortable with her outburst, but hardly surprised by it. He had planned to be out of the office earlier today, but a last-minute emergency required his immediate attention. He was not looking forward to a joyous arrival at home. But what now?

He follows her into the bedroom, where he apologizes and she talks about how inconsiderate he has been while he stands in awkward silence and waits for her to calm down and get over it. A short while after that, tired of this shopworn confrontation but with nothing resolved, they go ahead with their plans and try to make the best of their anniversary celebration.

See these two as a somewhat typical couple, each contributing to a troublesome marital pattern that neither wants to continue. His late hours at work trigger her dissatisfaction with him, which is understandable enough, but not something he wants to face when he returns home. And while she may not recognize it, her dissatisfaction contributes further to his overworking.

How does a pattern such as this become established? Perhaps more importantly, why does it continue? Let's look briefly at several milestones.

Beginnings. Just married and traveling to his first job, William and Diane stop for a late dinner. The restaurant is rustic on the outside but more elegant than they expected on the inside—and very expensive. The couple next to them orders the steak for two, which is the house special. On threadbare finances, the newlyweds must settle for two bowls of bean soup. Ashamed of his poor first showing as a husband, William eats in icy silence. Diane is unconcerned about their finances, but misses the easy conversation they usually share together. She invites him to talk about whatever is wrong, but cannot reach him, and so contents herself with her own dreams for the good life they will share together. She enjoys the bean soup.

On their first anniversary and for several years thereafter, he takes her back to this same restaurant, where they have the steak for two. It is his way of saying that he provides the good things in life for the woman he loves—and that he has made something of himself. She is not particularly fond of steak, but she goes along with it because it is important to him.

Already tangled into the fabric of their marriage are the strings of miscommunication, which will continue. By the time he achieves the financial success he requires of himself, the love and intimacy that these two cherished have been lost along the way.

Always Late. William's job requires long hours and occasional trips out of town—which he assures Diane is only until he gets established. Both miss the closeness of their college years, when they talked of their plans and studied together late into the night. Gradually, the work begins to consume him. The competition is intense and, as in most companies, the management appreciates hard work and places no limits on how much one is expected to do. Eager for responsibilities and unwilling to say no, William is soon overloaded.

Diane works too, but she expects a home life as well. After several especially long weeks, she is fed up. She knows his job is important, but she hardly sees him anymore. She asks her husband if he still loves her, and he assures her that he does. He understands her feelings, he says, and he promises that he will be home more and that they will do more together. And William means it—at least at the time. But he is already overcommitted at work and cannot seem to shake free.

Occasionally, when William arrives home several hours later than he agreed, it wreaks havoc with the meals Diane has planned. He is incredibly inconsiderate, she feels, and she tells him so. He accepts her anger, but he cannot control his schedule. If anything, he is late more often.

Why can't he give her a close estimate of when he will be home and then hold to it? When unexpected problems arise, he could phone. But she does not understand his long hours, and is angry when she hears he will be late again. So he grows reluctant to tell her just how late he will be. To maintain the peace, he commits himself to being home earlier than he knows is practical. When he gets caught with more work, as he often does, he cannot bring himself to call home and face her accusations.

Diane is justifiably angry when he arrives home so late, and she snaps at him or is calculatedly indifferent. She does not understand, and William, wanting to appear in control, has never confessed to her just how hard it is for him to manage his schedule. He would never let on that he is intimidated by her annoyance and hurt by her accusations. His job is reasonably satisfying, in obvious contrast to the marriage, which is by now quite unsatisfying.

The later he is, the angrier she is when he arrives, and the angrier she is, the more he prefers to remain at work.

And Then Children. The arrival of their first child furthers their alienation. The two experience parenthood quite differently.

Diane becomes calmer and turns inward when she is pregnant, nurturing the life inside her. William is stressed by the additional responsibility he feels for his growing family. He knows he should be especially supportive of her now, but it is a troubled time for him. He worries about the new bills, while his wife nurses their newborn.

Diane returns to work after a few weeks with her child, but it is a struggle for her. When she is away, her attention still lingers with her infant. She has to tear herself away each morning on her way to work. As is true for many new fathers, William's reaction is the opposite. He cannot wait to return to the office and convert some projects into job security and increased income.

The separation between the two continues to grow. Diane is consumed with the added responsibilities of the child, and she resents the absent father who should be present and involved and sharing the workload. William feels awkward as a father, but he notices the closeness between mother and child that he does not share. He feels like an outsider in his own family, and compensates for it by further losing himself in his job. The arrival of their second child adds not just a shave more trouble, as most parents expect; it more than doubles the workload while further stretching the finances.

Inadequacies and Misunderstandings. William judges himself as a provider, like many husbands, and is concerned that he is not measuring up. Although his earnings increase, every available dollar goes for something, leaving little in savings and no sense of permanent security. When he is not doing anything "productive" he feels worthless—as is typical of workaholics—and he often seems preoccupied when he has free time at home with the family. He cannot wait to get back in harness, to better provide for those he loves.

As his temporary ten- and twelve-hour work days stretch into years, Diane feels cheated of the conversation and closeness that were so important when that was all they had together. She finds it easy to resent his job, which owns more of him than a real mistress would. She feels she has a right to expect more out of a marriage, and is bitter over what is missing, overlooking what he does provide. More comfortable with expressing feelings than he, she lets fly with overflowing hurt and anger toward him. Behind her accusations is a heartfelt plea for him to notice that something is wrong. But he shows no recognition, and she complains he does not understand how she feels. Why does he seem to miss something so obvious?

Actually, he does not miss it at all. He sees her moodiness and hears her accusation, but does not respond in the way she wants. Too ill at ease with her to be comforting, he slips away to do what he does best. Financial success is a broadly recognized measure of a man, so regardless of her opinion, he feels he is upholding his main responsibility to his family.

But however much he accomplishes, he remains sadly insecure within himself, for something most basic is missing. He lacks real intimacy with another human soul who truly appreciates the life he is struggling to provide. The issue by now is not just the scheduling of time but the whole quality and meaning of their relationship.

Self-Perpetuation. Why do these two continue in the same unfulfilling routine, long after they can tell that it is not working? Such patterns have an intriguing force of their own, continuing in spite of our wishes to be rid of them. The reactions of each individual lead to the continuing actions of the other. His overworking contributes to her dissatisfaction, which contributes further to his overworking, and so on. Each step of the pattern leads to the next step, continuing in a circular fashion back to the initial step. The steps loop back upon themselves to form a vicious circle that maintains its own momentum. In this way, the pattern perpetuates itself (figure 1–1).

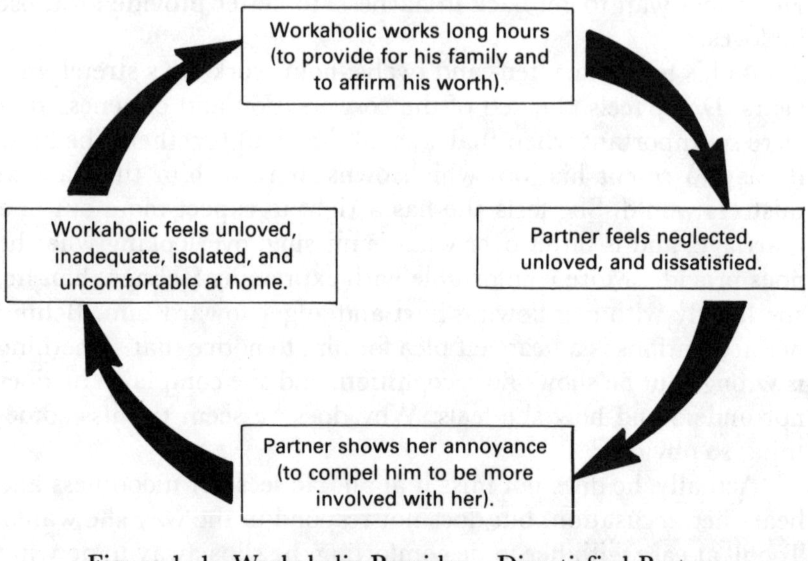

Figure 1–1. Workaholic Provider—Dissatisfied Partner
(*here, workaholic husband and dissatisfied wife*)

Unwitting Collaborators. Neither participant wants the pattern to continue, and neither is trying to maintain it. Each is acting for understandable reasons, in order to get something that he or she wants from the marriage. William wants to affirm his worth and to gain respect, while Diane wants more involvement. But their actions go wrong, failing in their reasonable objectives and contributing instead to the very problems they were meant to resolve. He is working harder in order to affirm his adequacy, but in so doing he provokes the very conditions in his marriage that make him feel less adequate. She shows her dissatisfaction with his overworking in order to get him to be with her more, but in doing so she adds to the pressures he feels to work harder.

While both contribute to the problem, they do so *unwittingly* rather than by intent. *Actions miscarry,* so that what we actually accomplish is often the direct opposite of what we are after. It is a conspiracy of mistakes, as intimates work together to maintain a pattern that neither wants to continue. It is through such unintended but quite understandable consequences that patterns perpetuate themselves.

Gender Positions. This illustration, and those that follow, portray the most typical ways patterns unfold in order to provide standard illustrations. Variations are also common. Men are more frequently workaholics than women, at least in terms of overworking outside the home, by perhaps a two-to-one margin. Adding the hours of child care and housework onto a regular job would qualify many more women as overworkers, of course, although not necessarily in the obsessive manner of true workaholics. Working mothers run nonstop because two jobs require twice the time, not because they have workaholic personalities.

Women who are workaholics can have similar patterns in marriages as workaholic men, with perhaps one variation. The husbands of workaholic women (or those that I have seen) are as likely to feel insecure and unhappy, but they are frequently possessive and overly jealous as well. Several called their wives frequently at work, requiring them to account for their whereabouts every moment, suspecting the wives of having affairs with bosses or co-workers. These women responded by taking on more assignments, to escape captivity and to be sure that they could support themselves on their own if necessary. Workaholic women may find more compatible pairings in fellow workaholics.

Identifying Patterns

Patterns are hidden traps that close on us while we are not looking, and then hold us against our will. We do not stay out of trouble by simply ignoring the traps, but by knowing the territory and learning to recognize the telltale signs of these traps. Nor do we get out of traps by struggling against the strength of their mechanisms. Once caught, we must look carefully and figure out how the trap opens. Only then can we apply our strength where it will provide the most leverage. As we become conscious of the traps in patterns, we see the choices hidden in them and the opportunities available to free ourselves from them.

Many of us are reasonably clear about what we want out of a marriage, but perplexed by why communications go wrong and why relationships fail. The illustrations provided herein show what the participants want from each other. Once you see what you are after, which is ordinarily quite reasonable, you can follow the loop to see the quirky ways that actions backfire.

The patterns presented in the following chapters are those that seem to occur most frequently in a wide range of marriages. While my listing is surely not exhaustive, it should provide a reasonable beginning.

I have tried to specify the main features of each pattern. If your own marriage fits a pattern, you should be able to see most of the main features—but not necessarily all of them. Each pattern you can identify adds something to your understanding of your marriage, so tag as many as seem pertinent. Some of the patterns share common principles. When patterns overlap, changing any of them can be helpful in changing related ones as well.

Read the patterns in any order you wish. You might begin with those that sound more interesting, or with whichever ones seem familiar and pertinent.

This book will show you:

- how you slip into troublesome patterns;
- how you act, quite unwittingly, to maintain them; and
- how, by awareness of these patterns, you can free yourselves to enjoy a more fulfilling marriage.

Stay with the Present. Some people argue, following the psychoanalytic tradition, that understanding one's past is the road to a healthy tomorrow. But is it that important? What can you do with it? A troubled past seldom provides the guidance we require for a more productive future. While one could learn to drive a car while looking in the rearview mirror, it would be slow and tedious at best and fraught with mishaps. It's better to look forward at where you are going, taking just an occasional glance backward at what is behind you. Begin with where you are now, and look ahead to where you want to go. The key to your future is already in your hands.

Since patterns exist in the present, they can be broken now by changes in your current attitudes and actions. Changing the critical aspects can and does alter a pattern, regardless of how long it has been with you. In some cases, taking the right steps can change patterns that have been lifelong aggravations.

In my therapy, couples often want to argue on and on about who said what last week, who did what to whom, and who was right. I try to refocus them onto what each of them means now, regardless of what was said; on what each can agree to do for the other today; and on how to make it turn out right.

Experiences with Patterns. Current interest in patterns runs high. These fascinating phenomena are variously termed interaction sequences, mutual reinforcement, accelerative feedback loops, causal chains, chain reactions, vicious cycles, or vicious circles. Under whatever name, they are considered in most of the current approaches to psychotherapy. While formal research is sparse, therapists are accumulating a wealth of insight and using it to find practical paths for changes.[4]

The patterns in this book organize both my own observations and those of other writers. As a clinical psychologist and a marriage and family therapist, I seek to collaborate closely with my clients. When I think I understand what is going on, I try to present it so that husbands and wives can see it as well. Spending hour after hour trying to explain myself forces me to clarify my own thinking.

These patterns are present in the ordinary problems of living common to many marriages. I am surprised by how many times I identify patterns for my clients, then realize afterward that I am doing the same thing in my own personal life. In my attempts to show others the sense they make, I come to understand myself better as well. The arguments I use to convince someone else can also apply to my own life. I do manage now and again to take some of my own advice, and to benefit from it!

2

Patterns Can Be Broken

ONCE we identify a pattern, we can change it. Merely understanding a pattern is a good beginning, for the inner workings that lock us into patterns can be reversed to spring us out of them. Merely identifying a pattern often involves a change of attitude, for we must admit to ourselves that we ourselves are a contributor to unwanted routines. This admission may be hard for some, but it is well worth it, for attitudes and actions must change together to change troublesome communications.

If you identify yourself in the pattern, the suggestions that follow apply to you directly. Marriage therapists might consider how the comments could be applied to couples in counseling.

Broadening Our Perspective. As things stand now between William and Diane, each feels it is the other one who is responsible for the schism between them and that any troubles he or she might be causing are relatively minor. William feels that a calmer and more cordial atmosphere is a requirement in this and in any marriage, and that it is Diane's emotional instability and continual complaints that are creating the strains between them. While he realizes his long hours at work cause some difficulties, he believes that earning a living is his top priority and that his wife should be willing to accommodate him. Diane, on the other hand, feels that intimacy is the heart of a relationship and that it is William's failure to be close to her that makes her feel unsatisfied. She does not recognize that she is hard to be around, and she believes that her distress is merely a product of his neglect, not a cause of it.

As in so many relationship conflicts, *what each wants is for the other to change*. She wants him to be home more and to be more open and more involved when they are together. If he would only change, she believes, she would have what she requires from the marriage. But he has his own wish list. Aside from wanting the financial security that he feels is his responsibility, he wants her to be more understanding of the pressures he is under and more tolerant of the hardships they cause. If she would only ease up, he figures, he would have an easier time with the marriage.

William and Diane must acknowledge that neither is the innocent bystander each claims to be. Both are unwitting participants in their unwanted patterns, and they must recognize their own contributions. Then some compromise may be in order. William might try to comply with her expectations to maintain the peace. Diane might find ways to be more satisfied with what she does have to lessen the pressure on him.

Compromise involves giving up something you want, which is admirable in principle but usually painful in practice. Nobody wants to settle for less. Any compromise should seem fair to both participants, but there will be problems if one is willing to compromise and the other is not. Fortunately, there is more to altering a pattern than lowering our expectations.

Examining Our Methods. Aside from compromise, and perhaps more fundamentally, what we need is a good method to go about getting what we want.

Our methods are both the heart of the problem and the backbone of the solution. Usually implemented intuitively and without conscious consideration, the wisdom of our methods produces the triumphs and failures of our lives. Anything we do is a *means* to try to get whatever it is we are after, and patterns reflect the means we use. Grasp that, and the importance of examining your means commands your attention.

We should try to be more conscious about the methods we are currently using and about our implicit beliefs that our methods should work. Diane might try stating her methods explicitly: "Expressing my dissatisfaction is my way to grab his attention," she might say to herself, "and if I do it long enough, he will have to become more involved with me." She might repeat it to herself, and examine it and see whether or not it is going to work for her. And William too might try stating his methods explicitly. "By working more," he could say to himself, "I can provide what a man must to fulfill his responsibilities." He too might try saying this to himself, and look at whether or not it is working for him. Only when we are truly conscious of our present methods can we grasp their meaning in our lives.

In unwanted patterns the methods being used are often counterproductive. We do not have to forget about what we want to improve in our relationships. More often, we must change our methods of going after what we want.

Tactics of Change

While it is easier when husband and wife work together to change, either one may rein in his or her contributions and thereby change the whole pattern. Since each step is required to close the loop, the removal of any one of the steps can break the whole pattern.

Since Diane is the more overtly dissatisfied of the two, she is more willing to acknowledge that a problem exists and to take steps to correct it. Workaholics like William tend to keep their feelings locked inside and do not open up to anyone about them. The typical overworker admits he has a problem only when his wife is about to leave him or after his first coronary, when his cardiologist tells him to slow down or else.

Some suggestions that might be useful in changing a pattern such as this one follow. Suggestions are presented here first for the wife, then for the husband.

What She Should Consider. The wife who seeks more involvement might try a two-phase plan. She should work to create a safer and more appealing atmosphere between the two of them; then build upon that to curtail his overworking. The principle is to use honey instead of vinegar.

Diane must try to befriend William in spite of his overworking. As long as he is wary of her, he is not very inclined to listen to her. Even her most minimal requests for intimacy he simply ignores or gives lip service, or makes a half-hearted try and then ignores.

While she has reason to be so often upset with him, her upsetness hardly helps solve any of their problems.

In counseling, she decides to try the opposite: to acknowledge how hard he works and to be grateful for the many things that he provides for the family. Showing appreciation for what he provides can lessen the pressure on him to overwork. Then, respected for what he provides, William would not need to take on more work to try to prove himself.

"I really do like our home," Diane says casually one evening. "I appreciate how well you provide for us." She talks about him more positively to the children and lets them know that what he does is really important. He is not sure how to interpret her change in attitude, but he is more inclined to listen to what she has to say.

Even though William is not talking to her about his concerns, she tries to convey to him that she understands them anyway. When he arrives home expecting to meet with the usual indifference, she tries instead to empathize. "It must have been a hard day," she begins. "You look worn out." It has been a hard day and he is worn out. But he hardly expected her to notice, and is pleasantly surprised.

She adds some charm and mystery and sensuality to support her request for more of his attention. She invests several weeks being warm and cheerful to him, then one day she really surprises him. She calls him at work and tells him she is fantasizing about him and that she is eager to see him even if he arrives home late as usual. Of course, her newfound fascination with him seems merely an act at first, planned in advance and performed before a willing audience. But she finds that she enjoys the act a lot more than she enjoyed the moodiness she had been feeling. And gradually, as she causes a stir, she comes to really feel the attraction she was pretending to feel.

By now, he finds coming home more pleasant, and he seems to genuinely want to please her. And when she requests more of his time, he is more inclined to listen to her.

But then further measures are required. While he is now attracted to his wife, he nonetheless remains tied to his work. Some leverage is needed.

Diane considers her options, then goes for broke. In good spirits by now, she tells her husband that she is tired of spending every evening alone and that she wants someone with her. Careful to be especially affectionate, she says she hopes that the someone will be him. She has his attention, and the message is not lost on him this time. He manages to free some time to be with her, which is pleasant for both of them.

Unfortunately, his newfound commitment lasts only until the next job crunch—a brief three days later. Fighting frustration, she has to recognize that lasting change takes time. She continues with her basic plan. She asks him about his work, without her previous tone of accusation, and really listens to what he says about it. She invites him to talk with her more openly about what both want from their marriage and what they mean to each other. When they are together, it is more involved and more pleasant. And gradually, he tries to plan his family back into his life.

Were the success of such programs guaranteed for every marriage, change would be quick and easy. But relationships are complicated, and changes take time. Most lasting changes require planning, trying something new, stepping back and taking another look, then more planning, then persisting in the program. Making lasting change requires a lasting commitment to change.

Obstacles may stand in the way, appearing as reservations or objections to the proposed changes.

Is It Manipulative? Is it manipulative to use tactics such as Diane's? Is it right to plan to be more generous, then shamelessly use it to get what you want? I do not consider any of the suggestions I make manipulative—at least, not in the unsavory sense of the word. *Manipulative* connotes using ploys that are unfair or underhanded that work to one's own advantage and against someone else's. Introducing warmth and charm into a marriage is neither unfair nor underhanded, because your partner must benefit in order for you to benefit. Changes that help both partners are wise and productive, not manipulative.

What Do You Have the Right to Expect? "Why should I have to change," Diane might ask herself, "to gain his love?" A wife may feel that she has a right to expect her husband to be involved with her and to love her for herself, as she is. She may feel it unfair that she should have to change herself in order to get him to give to her what he ought to be giving her anyway. Did he not promise to love and cherish her, for better or for worse? But is she being reasonable here? Whether or not she has the right to *expect* him to be more involved with her is a loaded question.

The word *expect* has two separate meanings. To *expect someone to be more involved* can mean to "anticipate" or to "figure" that he actually will be more involved. It can also mean to "demand" that he become more involved when he is not. This wife is not foolish enough to *anticipate* that he will be more involved with her than he actually is in the first meaning. Having the right to expect him to be more involved means that she has the right to *demand* it of him and the right to be upset or angry at him when he fails to meet those expectations.

Suppose that she does have a right to expect him to be more involved, and is therefore justified in being hurt and sullen and in taking it out on him when he fails her. She should first recognize that this is what she means by expecting more involvement from him. And she would do well to realize that just this and no more is what she gets out of her right to expect from him that which he is not inclined to do.

Most of us want more—sometimes much more—out of a marriage than we are getting. But we do not get it by expecting that which is not forthcoming. Sitting around with the right to expect something is not apt to produce it. If we see how short-sighted that is, we are free to try something productive. We must actively involve ourselves in making the realities of a relationship live up to our expectations of it.

What He Should Consider. Why would an overworking husband like William seek to be more involved with his family? The family provides him with a reason to work, but precious few personal satisfactions in staying at home. While work is gratifying, what other people call relaxation triggers tension in him, sometimes verging on panic. Obviously, something in his attitude must change before he will be inclined to change his behavior. And the overworking spirit can be quite tenacious indeed.

To be at all interested in changing himself, a husband like William must recognize that something is missing in his life that might be fulfilled within a family. He will have to consider how a closer marriage might benefit him and enrich his life. He will have to question himself: What does he want out of his marriage? Is it important enough for him to recommit himself to it? And he must see it as worth the time it would require and worth any sacrifices in his career advancement. But unless the advantages he foresees outweigh the sacrifices, he is not likely to do any changing. (Interestingly, one fellow I talked with claimed that after his marriage improved, he concentrated better at work and accomplished more in less time.)

When workaholics are facing their own mortality and are asked how they would have lived life differently, they seldom say that they would have tried to work more. Almost invariably, what they say is that they would slow down and take the time to be more involved with their families. They would want to learn about love and watch their children grow up. Surely some workaholics can learn this lesson before it is too late for them to do anything about it.

Perhaps most fundamentally, the overworker believes that only by working more can he insure a sound future for himself and his family. Overworking is for him a life insurance policy, to protect himself and his loved ones against unforeseeable financial catastrophes. But the policy does not insure his life at all, only that his passing will be easier on his beneficiaries. Overworking is not a way to resolve his fears but a way to run away from them. The overworking husband would do better to identify his fears and to acknowledge how tightly they control his activities.

In counseling, William decides to look more closely at his marriage to figure out what he wants from it and to take stock of what was left out. He realizes that he has been so involved in his job that he has lost track of what goes on at home. He knows he is now an outsider, with only a superficial understanding of his own family.

Although he was accustomed to functioning as a provider, he tries to see himself as more than a meal ticket for the family. He begins to pay attention to what goes on when he and Diane are together—how he feels, what he likes or could like about their interactions, and what he finds uncomfortable or annoying. Aside from simply spending more time at home, he tries to make better use of the time he does spend there.

Communicating more openly about himself with Diane is difficult, but he sees it is important for him to do it. He explains to Diane how important it is for him to provide sufficiently for the family. He expresses his concern that the future is uncertain and that an unexpected catastrophe could jeopardize his family's security.

William tells Diane that it is hard for him to break away from work when others are still working, and that he feels irresponsible when he has not done all that he feels he should do. He acknowledges that in spite of his achievements, he is helpless to command his own work schedule. He tells her that it is hard for him to relax, and that whenever he is not accomplishing something he feels worthless.

One who strives to appear strong is not inclined to mention his weaknesses. Talking to Diane about these limitations is hard, but William knows there is no other way for her to understand him. And talking about himself is a way to say that what goes on inside him matters and, more broadly, that *he* matters.

Calmly and with reasonable care, he mentions how he feels when she is dissatisfied with him. First, he simply tells her that he withdraws from her when she is annoyed. But that does not explain anything. It does not show her his underlying vulnerability or help her understand that he withdraws because he is hurt. So he goes on to explain that he interprets her dissatisfactions as additional pressure on him. Explaining his feelings in this way, he presents a more complete picture of himself that she can understand.

Diane has said she wanted him to be more open about his feelings, but the feelings he expresses to her now are not exactly the ones she wants him to be more open about. She did not want to hear that he finds her unpleasant to be around. But stating how he feels about the relationship is nonetheless a reasonable invitation to her to work with him to improve it.

He gradually becomes more comfortable with his position in the family, and he finds satisfaction in being more fully involved with them. He and Diane reach an agreement on how much financial security is necessary and where to limit the trade-offs on their time together.

More Objections. If you are an overworking husband like William, you may tender certain objections to programs for change such as his. You may feel that since your wife is pressuring you to be with her more, agreeing to do as she wishes is not a matter of your own choice. If your wife ices you for getting home late, you may not be able to rearrange your appointments to be home earlier without feeling that you are giving in to a form of emotional blackmail. You do not want to buckle under to her expectations, if that is how you see it—and still maintain your sense of independence and self-respect.

You would do better to interpret becoming more involved in your family as a sign not of weakness but of progress. Complying with a reasonable request shows flexibility and good judgment, even when one is being pressured to do so. An unwillingness to concede anything is more likely to indicate rigidity of character than strength.

Going against the Flow. The changes suggested here are difficult to make, for all the reasons that maintain the pattern in the first place. Consciously trying to change one's behavior can seem unnatural at first, because it goes against the flow. Both partners may feel that they are compromising themselves. Despite the progress Diane and William are making, Diane sometimes has a sense of abandonment and bitterness at the same time that she is trying to be more appreciative of William. She also has feelings that, while expressing appreciation for him, she is letting him get away with neglecting her. Meanwhile, for his part, William has to cope with his habitual sense that when he spends time with his family, he is wasting time that he should be using to earn a living. Moreover, he has to adapt to being involved again with this strange woman, his wife, whom he knows just well enough to know that she does not appreciate him as much as he would wish.

Any new game requires an ante up front. We must risk losing the comforts of our familiar patterns on the chance that the new and untried plan will be worthwhile in the long run. Giving in is not particularly appealing, nor is any giving that is one-sided with no guarantee of getting a fair return on the investment. The main incentive here may be knowing that the familiar pattern is a sure loser. A new plan can hardly do worse and could do much much better.

Perhaps in the spirit of compromise, we must each provide something the other wants in the expectation of gaining the benefits of goodwill, cooperation, and other things in return. Compromise itself involves much more than giving up something you want: it is better understood as a means to gain something that another must cooperate in providing.

In the best scenario, changes for the better can have perpetuating properties of their own. As Diane appreciates William more, he becomes more secure and more interested in spending time with her; as he is with her more, she finds it easier to appreciate him. Each step invites the next, forming a positive loop. As the new loop gains precedence over the old, the benefits accumulate and provide additional advantage. A new pattern gains momentum, now producing more satisfying interactions. These two channel a fresh breeze into what was previously a stale marriage.

The Work of Changing

Each of the patterns presented in this book is followed by suggestions for breaking the pattern. Not general tonics for whatever ails you, each of the prescriptions is matched to the specific problem. The steps in the pattern are like links in a chain, and each link is required for the chain to hold. The suggestions are intended to break one or more of the weaker links of the chain.

Can You Be Convinced? The field of psychotherapy is progressing, and many therapists today intervene more actively than people expect us to. No longer content to merely analyze problems, we look for ways to resolve the problems we uncover. What will it take to give up the old and to take the first steps into the new? I ask that question of each of my clients, and then I work with them to answer it.

Psychotherapy is an art of gentle persuasion. The task is not merely to suggest a change; that is usually the easy part. The real challenge is to convince people to try out the changes we might suggest. An active therapist seeks to understand why people object to changing, then to clarify their objections and allay their concerns. Using images, illustrations, catchphrases, and slogans can help make a point. Arguments I have found useful with my clients are also included in this book.

I have tried to make my observations as palatable as possible, yet I realize that some of the insights can be unsettling, as you identify yourself in a pattern and recognize that this is not your finest moment. Some resistance is normal. A friend of mine read my section on "the right to expect" someone to be more involved three times and told me that it was hard to understand. I said I would look at it to see if I could clarify it. But by the next day she had concluded that the problem was not in my prose but in her relationship. The material had hit her too close to home, she admitted, and had rattled her and left her confused. So if you find yourself troubled by the material in this book, or annoyed, or if you are merely lacking your usual concentration, the chances are that there is something in it that is important to you. Stay with it, and process your reactions. Be angry with me if you must, but above all, be honest with yourself.

Many of the suggestions I make will be obvious once you see them, while others will seem to go against the grain. Some will be easy and will yield immediate benefits, while others will produce limited changes at a slower pace. Most of the really meaningful changes will require your continuing attention, along with your commitment, persistence, and patience. Some of the suggestions may not be well tailored to your temperament, or that of your partner, so you may need to alter them or settle on a plan of your own that better suits your needs.

Suggestions made here that point you in the right direction may require outside assistance to properly implement them. Conversations with interested friends can help you identify and understand your patterns and help you support the changes you want to make. Consultations with a trained counselor can be invaluable. A summary of self-help studies in the journal *American Psychologist* concluded that the benefits of solo self-help are limited.[1] While individuals may change some on their own, they benefit more from the same suggestions when they have the support of a trained professional. A psychotherapist can provide an impartial assessment of your problems, experience in how new programs work, and the support to continue through the difficulties.

Marital partners seeking to make changes might want to join a marriage enrichment or marriage encounter program, or a church group that discusses marriages, or might visit with a marriage therapist. *The Binds That Tie* should be useful both to those in marriages and relationships and to those who work with them. Read about patterns, then collaborate to identify the patterns and to implement changes.

If you *are* a marriage counselor, you can read my suggestions as advice that you might give to those in these patterns whom you counsel. And in your personal life you might see yourself in some of the patterns as well.

Insight and Change. Realize that making any meaningful change will require your continuing attention. Insight and change have been said to proceed together through four stages.[2]

Initially, we act without insight into what we are doing. We know we have troubles, but we do not know what it is that we are doing that is causing the trouble.

In the second stage, we come to understand how we cause our own problems, but we are not able to identify our patterns in time. We act as usual, then see afterward that what we have done has caused problems.

In the third stage, we become more aware of the problems, so that we see what we are doing as we are doing it or slightly beforehand. But we still do it anyway. It is familiar. And in spite of our observations to the contrary, we still want to believe that we can get away with it just one more time.

In the final stage, we see the pattern beforehand, and having accepted the lesson, we avoid it. We are finally convinced that we are not exempt from the trouble involved, and we finally see that it is not worth it.

The process of change is not a blind leap to perfection. We must first understand ourselves and our partners, for only then will we see what to change. Since the journey is long, we must accept ourselves as we are and be tolerant of our follies. Otherwise, we nag ourselves so much that, in order to be free of our own criticisms, we become unconscious again. By understanding our follies, perhaps we will eventually become wise.

As long as we identify a pattern correctly and are trying to alter some of its steps, we can assume that we are on the right track. And when we are on the right track, it is usually worth it to persist.

Whose Job Is It to Change? As a marriage counselor, I hear both sides of problems, but only by splicing them together do I get the whole picture. The counselor's art is to understand each position and to be sympathetic to it without being taken in by it. One must avoid getting too tangled up in the arguments if one is to help others to untangle them. One must try to balance the concerns that women have about men against those that men have about women, then look for commonalities and areas for compromise.

Women seek counseling more often than men—about twice as often, meaning six or seven women are in counseling for every three or four men. Like most psychotherapists, I see more women than men in my office. I like to think that listening carefully to women has provided me with a nice balance to my own perspective as a man. My wife and partner, Nancy Davis, is a clinical psychologist who works primarily with women. Her commentary has helped balance the gender perspective in the patterns.

My hope is that by comparing the concerns of one partner with those of the other, patterns analysis can help both men and women see each other and their relationships more clearly. The concerns of each are best understood in terms of their interaction with the other. Just as it takes two to tangle, it takes understanding the two to untangle.

Some of the women readers of this book may be annoyed by my many suggestions for women but love my suggestions for their husbands. The men, in turn, may breeze over my comments for men but absolutely love my suggestions for their wives. Husbands and wives each love to hear lectures on how their mates should change—which is surely understandable but not particularly productive. If I sometimes offer a few more suggestions for women than for men, I ask the reader to take it in stride. My reason for doing so is that women are more apt to read this, or any, book on relationships, and they are more apt to try out the advice itcontains.

Change is easier to accomplish when both parties are willing to work together to change. Each contributes his or her fair share, and each supports the changes in the other. This arrangement meets standards of fair play. What husbands or wives want least is to have to make all the changes themselves. Nonetheless, since every step is necessary for the pattern to continue, either party changing at least one critical step on his or her own can effectively alter the whole pattern. If you cannot interest your mate, skip over all the arguments in between and look at the all-important bottom line: *The job of changing a relationship falls on the one who is more interested in the change,* not on the partner who is more stubborn or inflexible or less insightful. Since you are reading this book, the chances are that you are the one who is more interested in change. Interest your mate if you can, talk it over with friends if you wish, and tie in to a supportive community if it is available to you. Then go for it!

I hope that this book will help those of you who read it to better understand yourselves and your mates. I hope you will see a few ways to improve your marriage, and that you will have the wish to begin and the will to persist. And I also hope that through all the tangles and untangles, the two of you will share together in the love and commitment that make the struggle worthwhile.

PART

II

Tangled Connections

"Who's got whom?"

—colloquial

What would you put on a general list of the most troublesome areas in marriages? You might begin with the traditional squabbles about finances, as the control of the money signals power and standing. Many would mention the jumbled alliances among stepfamilies with two sets of children, which now replace the in-law problems of the previous generation. Some would include sexual incompatibilities—particularly those that are not simply reflections of other problems. Among the most harmful trouble areas are alcoholism and extramarital affairs. These latter two are so disruptive that it is fortunate that they are somewhat infrequent. Alcoholism ruins perhaps one in twenty marriages and is a factor in another one in twenty, leaving nine in ten marriages to other fates.[1] And while something over half of modern marriages will include at least one extramarital affair, the norm remains fidelity.[2] Affairs are generally infrequent and relatively unstable, so that even those partners who do stray tend to be faithful to each other more years than not.

Some of the more frequent concerns are much more mundane. Complaints about sharing the housework fairly are as typical in two-income marriages as they are among college roommates. Would it surprise you how many partners steam over who leaves a shirt on the favorite chair or who fails to take out the trash basket before it overflows?

Other concerns are harder to specify but are critical in spite of their apparent ambiguity. Particularly important are the widespread concerns over how much the partners are personally involved in and committed to the relationship. Issues of security or insecurity, of trust, of stability and commitment are involved here. How much does one rely on a joint venture that survives only on the willing approval of both partners? How much does one contribute to it, and how much does one expect in return? How much of oneself does one invest?

Husband and wife must find a balance between the cherished freedoms of two individuals and the commitments of the marriage. They must search for that subtle blend of independence and mutual interdependence, somewhere between the air to breathe and the ground to stand upon, between the wings to soar and the warmth of the nest at bedtime.

Attempts to establish that balance are fraught with confusion and are fertile grounds for self-perpetuating interchanges. Clear communication is especially important when issues are so sensitive and so unspecified. Miscommunication can leave partners perplexed by imaginary predicaments or talking across the table to an empty collection of rooms.

We look next at self-perpetuating areas of security, contribution, and involvement.

3

Insecurities and Reassurances

INSECURITIES and reassurances seem meant for one another. Announcing an insecurity acts to invite reassurance, and the reassurance is meant to soothe the insecurity that invited it.[1] But while reassurances sometimes do calm fears, just as often they miss the mark. Insecurities continue, inviting further reassurances that also fail to reassure, and so on.

Why is it that those who express their personal fears do not hear the reassurance they seem to be requesting? Ordinarily, they think their mates, who provide such easy answers, have not really heard the depth and the painfulness of their problems. The typical reassurance does not work because it does not seem to grapple with the full breadth of the concern. Our true insecurities are serious matters that have resisted our own best attempts to overcome them for quite some time. One who has really heard the problem, it seems, would not have such a quick and simple solution for it.

Here is one typical exchange. At the last moment and just ready to go out the door, Anna takes a last glance at herself in the mirror and is reminded by the reflection it offers that she is no longer as trim and youthful as she used to be. Frazzled already from too much running hither and yon and from too many chores requiring her attention, her mood takes a decided turn for the worse. Condensing the woes of middle-aged life into a single sentence, she offers a complaint, "I look fat in this dress!"

Since they are already late, the comment poses for her husband a problem that he feels he must resolve quickly. Robert responds, almost automatically, with his own quick fix: "You look fine!" he assures her, "You look lovely! Now let's go!"

But Anna is not reassured, nor should she be. Robert seems not to have listened to her at all. His reassurance was too quick and too easy. And he did not even glance at her before he answered—not even for a moment—to see whether she really looked good in the dress or whether it perhaps showed her weight too much. While his comment took the form of a reassurance, he seemed far away from her, dismissing her worries and ignoring her barely concealed plea for something more. She wants him to be more personal and more involved with her. But he is missing his cues, and his quick reassurance does more to confirm her insecurity than to allay it. Although trying to be supportive, he is directly contradicting her in her statements about herself.

Our natural response when we feel we have not been heard is to repeat ourselves. And that is what Anna does—only this time, with more volume: "I look terrible! I can't go looking like this!" She turns and heads back into the bedroom. With nowhere else to go, Robert follows, then waits helplessly to see how far into the tangle she will venture. He does not have long to wait. "You don't even care how I feel!" she accuses, a trace of tears moistening her eyes.

Already troubled by her insecurity and now stung by her accusation, he feels frustrated and quite irrelevant. Required to say something but wary of moving too close and getting burned, Robert chooses his words carefully. "I said you look fine," he argues. But his voice inadvertently betrays the annoyance that he is beginning to feel.

"You're mad at me," she responds quickly, and the conversation slides off the subject of appearances and onto a broader but equally unproductive rehash of who loves whom, as their miscommunication carries them both along.

Stubborn Insecurities. Insecurities can be stubborn and very sure of themselves. Look at an accomplished woman who is convinced she is foolish and unintelligent and who ignores any and all assurances from friends who find her bright and well informed.

"While I'm unintelligent," she seems to be saying, "I'm nonetheless smart enough to know that I'm not as smart as my friends say I am."

Versatile to a fault, insecurities can shadow almost any facet of life. Anna's complaint about appearances could just as easily have been a complaint about not being liked by her mother-in-law, about not fitting in or having no friends, about not having enough money to pay the bills, or about not going anywhere in a dead-end job with nowhere else to go.

Genders. In comparing the genders, I surmise that men have as many insecurities as women do, but are less inclined to show them. Men may be insecure about holding a job, meeting payments, falling behind, standing up for themselves, how they look, or how they perform sexually. Men are insecure about many of the same things women are insecure about, in other words, plus or minus a few variations. Women just tend to be more comfortable acknowledging shortcomings, while men usually conceal them for fear of appearing unmanly. So in patterns of insecurities and reassurances, women are more likely to mention their insecurities, inviting support, while men do the reassuring, becoming the supposed champions and advisors.

Men who do voice their insecurities frequently may invite rounds of futile reassurance. One man who feared he would lose his job mentioned it often to his wife. His job was safe, she constantly assured him, working hard to hide her own inner fears. Of course he sensed her fears, which only confirmed his own fears. This man was also afraid he would lose his hair, which was receding rapidly, and his wife always assured him that he looked fine anyway. But he felt she was not taking his fate seriously enough and he wanted more from her than that. Maybe he expected her to find a way to make his hair stay in!

But many men are not inclined to continue voicing their fears. One husband struggled daily with a job that he felt offered few opportunities for advancement and no recognition for anything exceptional that he might do. Responsible but usually uncommunicative, he took a chance one day with his wife. He told her that nobody appreciated what he was doing at work and that nothing was being accomplished there and that nobody cared. Wanting to make things better for him, she reassured him that his supervisors thought well of him. And if he didn't like the job, she assured him, he could quit. He didn't talk to her about his job anymore after that, although his feelings about it remained the same. He felt that it was something that his wife could not understand and should not have to worry about.

What went wrong here is what often goes wrong in such patterns. The reassurance she gave missed the mark, for he already knew that people liked him well enough. His concern was that nobody saw him as an outstanding worker and that there were too few ways to advance in the company. So her suggestion that he could simply quit the job showed no appreciation of the heavy responsibility he felt to provide for the family. He did not know what other jobs might be open for someone with his qualifications, and he was inwardly afraid that somewhere else, as the new man, he would have less job security than he had where he was now. So his insecurities were a bit broader than those he had mentioned. By reassuring him too quickly, his wife missed getting the whole picture.

Feeling understood is a requisite for the fulfillment of some more basic yearnings to be loved and appreciated for who we really are, faults and failings included. Trying to impress someone can be challenging, and succeeding at it can be a thrill on its own. But in the more complete and more lasting relationship that most of us expect from a marriage, we want to be understood and loved for what we are and not merely for the impression we can make.

Yet those who want simple understanding and support may fail to accept even the most honest assurances at face value, continuing to doubt themselves and to question those who reassure. Feeling basically unworthy and unacceptable, these people feel like frauds and pretenders who are merely passing as complete and worthwhile individuals. This so-called impostor phenomenon is better publicized in areas of career accomplishment and social standing, but it is just as prevalent in intimate relationships.

While women are more willing to admit insecurities, men seem equally inclined to undervalue reassurances. Men should look to identify their own attitudes in the illustration of Anna, to which we now return.

Discounting Any and All Assurances

Anna grew up in an aloof and unsupportive family, and now sees herself as an imposter. She adjusted to being considered a nuisance much of the time and to receiving frequent and sometimes caustic criticism from her mom or dad when they were in their typically sour moods. Not surprisingly, she came to see herself as inwardly incomplete and obviously unworthy of being cherished. Like so many children, even children who rebel and challenge their parents, she unconsciously accepted her parents' pronouncements of her basic and fundamental inadequacies. She became a compulsive pleaser, trying against all hope to win their love, although nothing she did or could do was ever enough. She concluded, not surprisingly, that she was not good enough.

Fortunately, Anna happened to form a relationship with an easygoing fellow who liked her pleasing manners and her modesty. Robert was eager to marry her, although she always felt that she was not what he really wanted. And after the marriage, he continued to want her, which was a source of worry and confusion for her. She knew she was not worthy of being loved and yet this odd man, her husband, appeared to be doing many of the things that would indicate that he loved her. How could she reconcile the one with the other? Those who feel unworthy are ill prepared to rearrange their perspective to see themselves as worthwhile. Unfortunately, there are other easily available options. The supposed impostor will usually use each of these options at various times, as Anna does.

Fooled. Especially in their first years together, Anna figured that she had Robert fooled into believing that she was as wonderful and charming as she worked so hard to appear. But an actual impostor is not entitled to the love and comforts of a marriage. At any time, she feared, Robert might find out that she was just junk, and once he found out, her charade would be over. Once he realized she was not a proper wife but an impostor, he would surely turn his back on her and she would be on her own.

When he finally figures out she is a fraud, she fears, she may not be prepared for it. She does not want to sit idly by and wait for it to befall her. Rather than be taken by surprise, she takes the initiative herself. She tries to tell him that she is unworthy—that she is a wreck on the inside and flawed on the outside and much worse off than she appears. She portrays her insecurities in full breadth and vivid color but to no avail. The unworthiness she sees in herself is not easily translated into anything that appears wrong to her husband. Robert concludes that she is just insecure or that she has a poor self-concept, and works to reassure her that her concerns are unwarranted. So the case of the fraudulent marriage continues unresolved.

Just Being Polite. Anna tries another interpretation. She figures that Robert surely sees through her by now, but is just being nice to her because he feels he must. In reality (she surmises), he shares the same low opinion of her that she has of herself, and only obligation and social proprieties conspire to prevent him from saying so. So in this scenario she is not the one who is the impostor—he is! Robert is the one who seems false, toying with her feelings and pretending to think well of her when they both know that the assurances he gives are not genuine.

So Anna ignores his compliments or is uncomfortable with them, seeing them not as genuine support but as mere social amenities. She does not appreciate being treated so superficially, and she anticipates what will happen when he finally says what he really thinks of her. She is impatient with the politeness, yearning to find out where she really stands with him so that she can go on from there. So she reiterates her insecurities, spells them out, asking him to take her seriously and deal with her shortcomings honestly. But he deals with them the only way he knows how, at least for a while, by assuring her that really she is wonderful in the ways he says. Her insecurities remain—it is only their trust in each other that is weakened.

A Real Nobody. Anna begins to interpret his easy acceptance of her as a statement of his own obviously uncritical standards or low social standing. It is too easy to perceive those who judge us critically to be superior beings looking down upon us from on high, but to take for granted those who readily accept us for whatever we are.

Groucho Marx captured the paradox of this in his quip "I wouldn't want to belong to a club that would have me as a member."[2] To the woman looking at her ordinary and perhaps unremarkable husband, this becomes, "I would never respect a man who would be pleased with no better than me as his wife." To the man looking for the perfect woman, it is, "I could never respect a woman who would settle for me as her husband."

A common interpretation of the quip is that Groucho was showing a poor self-concept, which I suppose might be so. But look closer. The actual target of contempt is not Groucho but the club itself, whose standards and social standing are so poor it would accept someone like Groucho as a member. Any club that accepts him thereby discredits itself, and Groucho is too good to belong to a club with so little class.

Similarly, the man who is willing to settle for Anna appears to her to have low standards and poor judgment, and he obviously lacks what it takes to find someone better. Merely by accepting her, Robert discredits himself, and Anna remains unimpressed and even somewhat cynical or contemptuous of him. And since she has so little respect for him, his reassurances can hardly count enough to bolster her own opinion of herself. That he continues to want her discredits him further in her eyes. She remains insecure herself, unimpressed by him or by his uncritical judgment.

Three Strikes and You're on Your Own. So at various times Anna sees herself as an impostor who has Robert fooled, or sees him as just being polite and fooling her, or concludes that he must be a "nowhere man" to settle for a wife no better than herself. Along with her own feelings of worthlessness, she is overly inclined to see someone who accepts her as imperceptive, phony, or worthless. A poor opinion of oneself cannot be taken to indicate a high opinion of others. In these ways Anna discredits the appreciation she receives so that Robert's opinion of her cannot matter. She therefore remains insecure in the face of what would otherwise count as reassurance and support.

In similar ways, too many of us discount the approval of those around us. We maintain poor images of ourselves in spite of our real accomplishments and regardless of our apparent popularity.

Anna was perhaps lucky to match with a man who was so supportive. Unfortunately, many men and women who are uncomfortable with approval pair too easily with contemptuous and sometimes even abusive mates. Discounting the truly accepting person as shallow or too easy, they perceive the one who is arrogant and critical of them as having more substance. Those who cannot accept approval are attracted to what they perceive as the honesty of the partner who disapproves. So they find themselves facing the same contempt they knew previously, which merely maintains their basic sense of inadequacy.

Insecurities Obligate. Insecurities obligate reassurance, and those who continually portray their insecurities may do so not to resolve anything but to obligate someone else to take care of them. When Anna complains that she is overweight, she is not trying to resolve the problem quickly and get on to other things. Feeling overwhelmed, she is passing the responsibility for her unhappiness onto those around her, especially Robert.

On a quiet evening at home, Anna worries to her husband that she has no friends. Frustrated by her insecurities, Robert pushes hard for a solution. "People do too like you if you would only give them a chance! Why don't we go to the club tonight?" he suggests. "I'm sure you would feel a whole lot better."

"Yes, but—" she begins, and then completes the sentence with a handy but quite plausible excuse not to do anything. "Yes, but I never like those places with so many people gabbing and gabbing and never saying anything."

So he suggests something else, and again she has a plausible reason to hold her ground and not let him push her into going. He tries to coax her along, but nothing he does makes her feel any better. And while they argue over whether she has any friends, whether she looks all right, and whether to go out and where, the two of them do agree together on one fundamental thing when all is said and done: they agree that he is the one who carries the responsibility for her unhappy life. The more responsibility he assumes for her, the less she assumes for herself, and both are the worse for the trade-off.

Insecurities Influence. Most insecurities are not so imperialistic, but even the more modest varieties affect both partners in a relationship. The one who is obligated to do the reassuring is not necessarily pleased by these proceedings. Taking on the responsibility for her feelings, Robert finds himself unable to do or say anything to improve things. All the reassurance he can provide does no good, and he feels ignored, irrelevant, frustrated, and then angered by his powerlessness. While her insecurities obligate reassurance, at least for the moment, the futility he experiences annoys him and leads him to withdraw emotionally from her.

In addition, as in many marriages, the picture Anna presents of herself strongly influences Robert's opinion of her. The woman who presents herself as confident and attractive tends to appear that way to her partner, while the one who presents herself as a physical, social, and intellectual misfit is likely to be seen as such. When Anna complains that she looks fat in one dress or another and points out the bulges, she convinces Robert much more than he is willing to let on. Even as he continues to reassure her, he comes to see her as noticeably overweight, just as she claims she is. Unwittingly, she is painting a picture of herself in his mind that will linger long after their conversation. He finds himself less and less attracted to her, and it begins to show. He is attentive only when she demands it, and his reassurance is only a mere formality and not heartfelt. So by now his reassurance is indeed false, just as she suspected all along.

Paying too much attention to her flaws and failings undermines her own confidence in herself as well. As Anna bad-mouths herself, she too comes to believe her own propaganda. And she observes that Robert is no longer so interested in her, provoking further insecurities and obligating further reassurance. The pattern perpetuates itself (figure 3-1).

Why Care about Approval Anyway? Vulnerable already, people who are insecure are especially rattled by others' negative opinions of them. Criticism hurts, as does being ignored or unappreciated, and even relatively good marriages have troubling misunderstandings or cross words and stubborn wills pulling at cross purposes. So it is understandable that insecure individuals seek to insulate themselves from the opinions others have of them.

Following the popular adage to look to oneself for confidence, many individuals try to downgrade the importance of their social networks. Concluding that they care too much about approval,

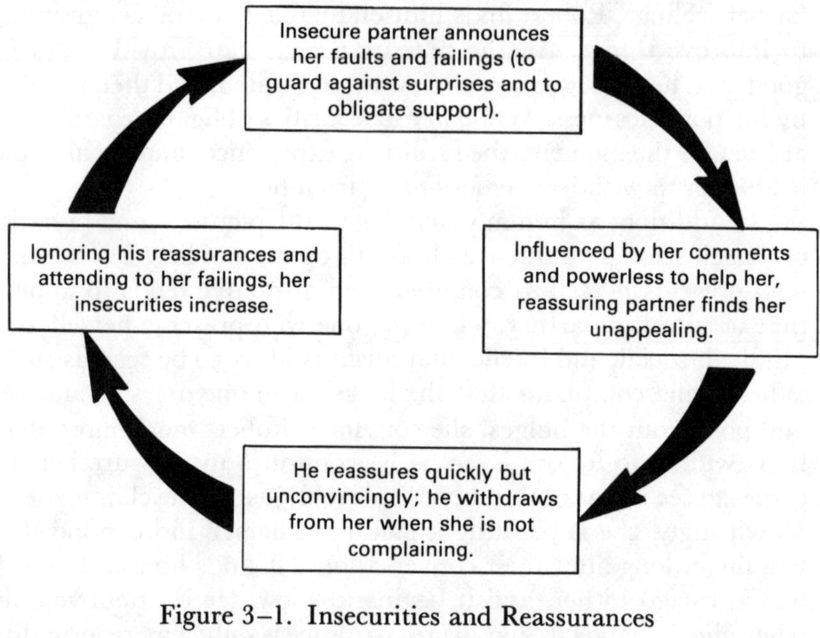

Figure 3–1. Insecurities and Reassurances
(*here, insecure wife and reassuring husband*)

they seek to rely more on themselves and less on the support of friends and family. But it fails to allay their insecurities.

A robust confidence in ourselves is surely important, but ignoring the support that we do receive is a poor way to gain confidence. Those who think they care too much about approval are probably misunderstanding themselves and making things worse by their attempted solutions. Commonly, *the problem is not that they care too much about approval, but that they care so much about avoiding disapproval*. The support they do receive matters little, and does not bolster their confidence or make them feel appreciated.

Negatives are often felt more than positives, and the insecure are the most strongly affected by criticism and rejection. A closer look reveals that their striving for approval is mainly a means of avoiding disapproval. Insecure people seek to please not because they find it satisfying to do so but because they are afraid to displease. Unfortunately, their positions remain precarious. Disapproval lurks ready to strike, regardless of how much approval they accumulate. And their solution—which is to care *less* about approval—further isolates them from the support that might outweigh the inevitable adversities. Ignoring any approval they receive, they are still badly unsettled by the disapproval.

So if you have a generally supportive marriage, the solution is not to care less about what you have but to care more. Consider love and assurances to be solid staples in any good marriage. Learn to see them more clearly and to nurture and cherish them.

Here's how.

Confidence Is Contagious

Those who feel inherently unworthy might examine more closely the qualities on which they judge themselves wanting. An actual impostor pretends to be something, but lacks the social requisites needed to qualify as genuine. If you believe yourself to be a fraud, what is it that the authentic players possess that you are lacking? What must one have to be lovable, or merely acceptable, that you do not have? Be conscious of whatever vague feelings you have, and try to capture them in words.

Someone like Anna should realize that other quite ordinary and respectable people occasionally feel like impostors too. Merely feeling like a fraud is actually quite normal and cannot in itself make her what she fears she is.

Many of us have had critical years in our lives when we felt inadequate, excluded, and unloved—and therefore unlovable. Such experiences can leave us with feelings of being misfits and outsiders, and such feelings are not easily assuaged by better times later on. We identify so strongly with our prior limitations that we cannot accept our current fortunes at face value. Circumstances mold identity. Being unloved translates into feeling unlovable; being unappreciated suggests worthlessness; scorn suggests we have done something shameful. Constant anger and criticism directed at us is justified only if we are wrongdoers.

If you were treated as a burden as a youngster, it is understandable that you feel like a burden in your marriage. But you must realize that the problem was in your family of origin. It is not a permanent quality that must follow you into your new family. In a marriage, you begin almost from scratch to create a new place for yourself in the eyes of your chosen partner. To be as good as you appear, you need only the confidence to follow through on it.

As adults, we have much greater power to shape our relationships. Understanding how opinions of us are formed, we can work to create the opinions that we want others to have of us.

Those who parade their insecurities must realize that whatever reassurances they thereby pull from others will never be sufficient to ease their qualms. Confidence must come from inside themselves and from their trust in the support they receive from those close to them.

If you are insecure, try as much as possible to curtail repetitive complaints about yourself. Find something else to say.

A Little Help from a Friend. Insecure individuals might ask family and friends to remind them when they begin to rerun their same old negativities to help them remain conscious of what they are doing. Anna might acknowledge that she has a problem of being carried along by her insecurities and ask her husband to mention it to her whenever she winds back into them. A gentle reminder should suffice, such as, "You are being really harsh on yourself."

The overly reassuring husband is also an active participant in perpetuating this pattern, and he should help alter it. Frustrated by his interactions with his wife, he may be highly motivated to try a reasonable alternative.

Since his habitual reassurances unwittingly serve to perpetuate the pattern, curtailing the reassurances could help greatly. While reassurances are meant to convey confidence, too many of them can just as easily suggest a lack of confidence. Too much reassurance implies that the wife is indeed unstable, and that only his own continual attention maintains her fragile mental balance. Were it not for his support, Robert fears, his wife would come unraveled, and he would bear the burden for her tragic breakdown.

Robert has bought the façade and confused it with reality. To help Anna, he must believe that someone of substance resides behind all her complaints. He must find the confidence to respond more honestly in order to jar them both loose from their repetitive interchanges.

I would advise Robert to merely listen to her fears and show that he understands, instead of giving the same mindless reassurances. An excellent way to do this is to simply reflect back the feelings and concerns that someone expresses. So when Anna says, "I look fat in this dress," Robert responds, "You feel it doesn't look good on you. I hear what you're saying."[3]

This seems simplistic, which it is, but it serves a purpose. It shows her that he is listening, which is important. And he avoids the decidedly unempathic appearance of giving the usual quick but facile fix.

"I hate looking like this," Anna continues.

"I know that how you look is important to you," Robert responds, showing that he is listening.

"It's just that I'm getting older," she admits, now suddenly saddened by her own realization. "And it shows too much."

"I think I can understand that," he acknowledges. "We're both getting older."

This reflection of feelings provides an opening for further communication between them on more personally sensitive subjects. She feels genuinely understood, and that in itself is comforting and takes the edge off some of her fears. By merely listening Robert leaves the problem on her shoulders, where it belongs, and shows that he has confidence in her that she can solve it herself. The friend who has truly understood a problem is in a much better position to offer reassurances and is more likely to have them turn out to be helpful.

Those who condemn themselves may be shocked to hear the acid of their own words reflected back at them. The woman who says "I look awful!" is not at all pleased to hear someone respond by saying, "You feel you look awful?" or "Do you really?" While she is willing to complain about herself, she is unwilling to hear others do so.

I find that even chronic complainers stop complaining rather abruptly when someone provides them with a reflection of their own prejudices about themselves. One visibly attractive woman complained bitterly that she was ugly, pointing out apparent flaws in her features, while her frustrated husband continued to contradict her in order to reassure her. But arguing with her was obviously not the answer. In my office these two began their typical interchange. "Is there a place in this world for ugly people?" I asked her naively. My question slapped crosswise at her vanity. "I'm not really ugly!" she shot back angrily, wasting not a moment in correcting me on this most important matter. By mirroring her statements back to her, I had short-circuited the usual chatter, and she did not like what she heard herself saying. When insecure people can no longer force others to carry their insecurities for them, they must carry its burden themselves or drop them by the wayside.

"The truth shall set you free," it is said, although we should add that at first it's going to hurt a little. We must be prepared for a few strains along the way to more honest relationships.

Robert has assured his wife over and over again that he loves her, yet Anna was never convinced, nor could she have been. No one believes protestations of love spoken under such obvious duress. I advise Robert to introduce a measure of honesty into the ruckus. The next time Anna complains that he does not love her, he admits to her that at times like these, he does find it very frustrating to be with her. She is upset and angered by this unexpected turn and remains miffed for several hours. But she does not continue pushing her tired old question. His answer was not what she wanted to hear, but at least it was honest. Over the following weeks, Anna and Robert come to better understand what they can and cannot expect of each other.

When should one reflect simple understanding, and when is it appropriate to reassure? Generally, try to understand first, and *then* support and reassure. Obviously, it is better to seek to understand a problem before you try to solve it: otherwise, you may provide a solution to the wrong problem. Moreover, go with what works, and stop what does not work. Whenever Robert reassures again and again to no avail, he must realize that something is amiss and try instead to understand the problem. In contrast, one whose reassurances are accepted and appreciated is on the right track and should continue.

An Act of Confidence. Perhaps the surest way to increase your self-confidence is to act as if you had the confidence that you wish you had. By acting confident, you convince others of it and convince yourself as well. Change your outward conduct and your inward attitudes are apt to change too. "Fake it until you can make it" is good advice from Alcoholics Anonymous. "You can be as brave as you make believe you are" suggested Rodgers and Hammerstein in *The King and I*.

Pretending to have confidence in oneself will seem false and insincere to those who have lifelong insecurities. That which is more familiar is apt to seem like the real you, while the confidence that breaks the pattern feels awkward, false, and merely an act. Never mind—*do it anyway!* Those who avoid doing anything that does not feel completely familiar and natural restrict themselves to doing only what they have always done, and they stay in the same old ruts. Appear to have confidence long enough, and confidence will become a familiar friend to you. Wear it well, and what you wear will come to feel like the real you.

Paradoxical as it seems, showing confidence in oneself can be scary if you are not accustomed to it. Those with optimistic outlooks take risks and are vulnerable to jolting disappointments, while pessimists take no such risks. Dwelling on fears and doubts, while unpleasant, feels like a reliable way of preparing oneself for the worst. The motto of the insecure seems to be, "Blessed are they who expect nothing of themselves, for they shall not be disappointed."

Taking such precautions is clearly shortsighted. Optimism does leave one vulnerable to disappointments, but its cumulative gains far outweigh the occasional reversals. And while pessimism lowers the risk of unexpected failure, its price is a routine joylessness that is barely more tolerable than the worst case against which it guards. It's better to take a risk on a possible win, than to settle for the security of a certain loss.

Confidence in Your Marriage. It's important for each partner in a marriage to contribute some confidence in the journey that the two of them are taking together. Husbands and wives look to each other for some assurance that their life together is worth the years that they are committing to it. A marriage tethered to fears and negativity hardly seems worth the required sacrifices. The confidence you show in a marriage suggests strength to take care of whatever comes along, satisfaction with your partner, and trust in the future you are building together. Confidence is contagious, and you will see the confidence you show in yourself reflected back in the eyes of your partner.

It may be surprising how strongly perceptions are swayed by how one presents oneself. The wife who sees herself as warm, or wise, or well liked vastly increases her chances of being seen that way by her husband. Even apparently obvious characteristics like physical attractiveness are still very much a matter of perception and are subject to social influence. A woman who conveys an easy confidence in herself may convey a charm and mystique that men find appealing without quite knowing why. A man who shows confidence in himself conveys a sense of strength and security that most women find appealing.

A woman who wants to show a more positive side of herself might focus on something she does like about herself. Anything will do, although it may feel safer to begin with something unimportant. If nothing comes to mind, no need to give up. A friend can usually mention more than a few good qualities. Then mention one of them in passing.

Anna makes up her mind to be more optimistic. "How about this for a suntan?" she remarks after years of feeling awkward about her body. "Does this look good, or what!"

Accustomed to hearing only complaints from her about her appearance, Robert does not know what to make of her. He says nothing, but a good impression lingers.

Backtracking on her years of insecurity, Anna chooses her openings and sprinkles in a selection of favorable comments about herself. In so doing, she fabricates for herself a new identity. Puzzled by her new confidence, Robert begins to wonder if there is something more to her than he saw before. For the time being, she has created a smidgeon of mystery about herself.

Anna finds that her simple self-affirmations fare just as well in more substantial matters. She mentions that she is loyal to her friends and likes that about herself. At another time, she notes that she is patient with their children, and funny.

A more confident Anna informs her husband, "I am the greatest wife you ever had." He could hardly argue the point, as she is also his first and only wife. He has to smile at her foolproof packaging.

My own wife assures me that it will be fun being older together. I cannot say that I am ready to relinquish my fantasy of everlasting youth or that I savor the prospect of old age. But I genuinely appreciate her vote of confidence in our future.

A Willing Audience. Should it surprise anyone that such comments are easily accepted by husbands? Many people avoid saying anything positive about themselves, for fear they will appear boastful or someone will contradict them and put them in their place. And among supposed friends who are nonetheless competitive with one another, this does happen. But husbands and wives rely on each other for the fulfillment of their marital fantasies. Each *wants* the other to be something special. So your partner is a more-than-willing audience for whatever charms you can weave from loose threads or pull out of thin air. Any husband is apt to appreciate his wife's confidence in herself and to gain some confidence in her. Regardless of whether he truly believes everything she says about herself, he will usually go along with her. Her optimism releases him from the burdens of providing the confidence, and besides, it would be poor manners to contradict her! The longer he goes along with it, the more familiar and natural it all seems.

Some who show new self-confidence receive no immediate feedback and interpret that to mean rejection. But usually, it only means that the upbeat comment took the partner quite by surprise and left him or her with no inkling of how to respond. Or perhaps the partner simply agreed and saw no need for comment. Making a good impression need not provoke an immediate reaction; the benefits may trickle in slowly in small ways over the following weeks. You may have to look closely to see the indications, but do look for them, for they are lurking out there waiting to strengthen the new confidence you have in your own confidence.

Teamwork. While insecurity-and-reassurance patterns can be broken by either partner, the best changes occur when both work together. Reassurances can allay insecurities, but only under the right circumstances. They must be based on a genuine understanding of the problem; they must be honest and sincere; and the one receiving them must see them as sincere and important.

With those I counsel, I try to be as supportive as I can be and still maintain my credibility. What should I say to support an individual who feels that anyone who does support her is being false or foolish? Having to cover both bases at once, I limit myself to giving guarded compliments: "I would say that you are doing all the right things there, but if I did you would lose your respect for my opinion."

If you are pestered by insecurities, you can shake free of them. *Notice when you discredit approval; then learn to take it more seriously.* Keeping a written record, such as a journal, can help. Over several days, observe and tally every time someone is supportive of you; then write down your reaction to it. Note whenever someone is complimentary or simply friendly to you. Also tally any time someone is critical and write down your reaction to that as well. Then see if you are allowing the support you receive to count less than the criticism. Consciously try to place more importance on the reassurances you receive. When you receive a compliment, try to at least look at the person who gave it to you and return a warm "thank you!" for it. Also, try to downgrade the weight you give to your shortcomings. As much as possible, focus on your successes and minimize your failings.

Absorbing approval is very good for your outlook on life. Investigators conclude that popular personalities are more apt to seek approval and be pleased by it, but are not particularly concerned about criticism.[4] By contrast, those who have problems with social relations tend to be overly sensitive to criticism, while they ignore approval and are uncomfortable with compliments. The implications are clear. Paying more attention to the positives of your social relations should help you become more comfortable with yourself and better liked by those around you. Caring about approval is good for you and good for your marriage as well.

Other research confirms the importance of having a positive outlook. A study of some 220 married individuals showed that having confidence in oneself contributes significantly to overall marital satisfaction.[5] Self-confidence not only makes you happier with your marriage, it makes your spouse happier with you.

So confidence is truly contagious. Those who can appreciate the confidence others have in them are strengthened to convey confidence in return, breathing renewed hope into a life together.

While optimism should be appreciated, nobody should expect a steady regimen of it. Life is often troubling and confusing, and husbands and wives want to be able to share their concerns and find love and support in each other. Recognize that it is not simply the expression of insecurities that causes problems, but the failure to accept support that is offered. Most husbands and wives are willing to listen, and they want to be helpful. When insecurities are genuinely understood and the support offered is accepted, they feel closer to each other and surer about their marriage. Acceptance of reassurance conveys wonderful confidence in the one who gave it. The one who needs the assurance can be grateful for the help, and the helpmate can be grateful for the satisfaction of providing help that is well received.

You can be sure you are on the right track when a problem-solving conversation finishes with, "Thanks for listening. You are always a big help." A warm hug is a good sign as well.

4

Pursuers and Distancers

The change women want most is for men to talk about their feelings, and the change men want most is to be understood without having to talk about their feelings.

— a recent survey[1]

WHEN people marry, they assume that the question of their basic personal involvement is finally settled. It is singles who must face mismatched expectations as they try to sort through who they want and who wants them. The singles routine is a chase in which previously independent partners conspire to adjust to each other and to commit themselves or remain at odds. One partner may be infatuated, while the other takes it all for granted. One may push for more involvement, while the other feels too crowded. Individuals who are committed to having romantic adventures stay interested only as long as the challenge persists.

But married people seldom expect the hide-and-seek of the singles' life to follow them into marriage. A marriage bonds two lives together as one, and is supposed to settle the basic questions of the couple's involvement with one another. The problem is that it seldom plays out that way. Married people actually experience many of the same crossed expectations that people in courtships do, so that many continue to relate as "pursuers" and "distancers."[2] Since marrieds are often together almost continually outside of working hours, a new problem looms before them: how much do they have to say to each other?

Among the most typical dissatisfactions in marriages, expectations about the level of mutual involvement are surely near the top of the list. One partner wants more communication and more closeness and pushes for it, while the other wants more freedom and slips away just out of reach.

Mismatched Expectations

When they arrive home in the evenings after work, Don and Paula have their own independent if somewhat typical expectations of married life. Both have been at the office doing paperwork, attending meetings, and managing relationships with easygoing officemates and with some seemingly impossible ones as well. Both are worn out and want to relax and unwind. But it is how they choose to relax that is different. Paula wants to sit down together in the living room with some cheese and crackers and wine and rehash the trials and triumphs of the day. She wants to talk about who did what to whom and how everyone felt and what happened next. But Don wants to sit in front of the television with a cold beer and forget about the office, of which he has had his fill for the day. He wants to watch the news or sports or just flip through the channels—to put his mind on cruise control, with no obligations to do more.

In a catchy cartoon, two sweethearts sit together on a park bench, she on his lap. Both are fantasizing about married life.[3] The woman envisions the two of them going out for dinner in formal attire, with the maître d' showing them to a table. But the man sees himself at home in front of the television in jeans and an old shirt, with his sweetheart cheerfully bringing him a glass of beer. Actual married life will hold surprises for both of them.

Even aside from their different preferences for relaxation and other activities, two partners may also differ on the sometimes confusing question of how and how much they want to be involved. One partner wants more conversation and more real communication, particularly on personal subjects such as feelings and the nature of the relationship. For this partner, more openness, more sharing of each other's lives, and a greater sense of intimacy are all high priorities. The other partner, however, feels awkward in intimate conversations, even wondering what to say. The two are apparently close enough already, it seems, and this partner's preference is to put more breathing room between them and to have a greater sense of freedom.

Who Wants More Sharing? Men and women tend to differ in their inclinations to share the personal sides of themselves. Women are often more comfortable expressing their feelings and are likely to want more communication, indeed more intimate and more intensely personal communication. Probably the most frequent complaint women make to marriage counselors and sympathetic friends is that their husbands or sweethearts do not talk to them or seem closed off from them. Many men, in turn, seem awed by their wives' requirements for more conversation. They are unsure of what to say or are sure that they have nothing to say, and they are more comfortable remaining silent, perhaps on the grounds that anything they say can and just might be used against them. So in this chapter on "pursuers" and "distancers," I take the liberty to portray the woman as the pursuer and the man as the distancer.

Of course, for some couples these preferences for intimacy are reversed. Sometimes it is the man who wants to be more personal and the woman who wants to stay removed. In these cases, the reader should simply reverse the gender positions in the illustration I provide.

Is More Communication Better? When approximately four hundred psychiatrists were asked to list the major reasons that marriages fail, an impressive 45 percent of them said that the primary cause of modern divorce is the husband's failure to communicate his feelings.[4] (Only 9 percent blamed sexual incompatibility.) These psychiatrists faulted the husbands for insufficient communication, not the wives for expecting too much conversation. And indeed, sharing oneself is important. A whole generation of supposedly strong and obviously silent husbands must learn to do more of it or face the consequences. The psychiatrists surveyed are probably representative of most people in the helping professions, who generally cherish intimate communications and prescribe it to fix relationships. They are naturally sympathetic to those who reach for more closeness, and they see one's failure to express oneself as an obvious handicap in any intimate relationship.

I am sympathetic to this view, too, but I think it is too easy to presuppose a sacred connection between how much we communicate about ourselves and the quality of our marriages. A vast collection of social science research fails to find any such connection. In fact, many studies find *no connection at all* between the *amount* of communication and the level of satisfaction reported in a relationship. They find solid marriages in which relatively little is said between husband and wife, and marriages in which constant expressions of genuine but antagonistic feelings simply promote animosities. The proposition that greater expression of feelings promotes marital satisfaction is strictly a myth.

Unfortunately, the myth is widespread. One survey found that 75 percent of some 280 unmarried undergraduate students agreed that increased self-expression, whether positive or negative, enhances marital satisfaction for both partners.[5] Belief in this myth, however, has serious consequences. Those who believe that all communication is good are often quick to provide negative expressions and do so self-righteously, thereby tearing at the fabric of what they are supposedly trying to preserve.

One group of investigators closely observed and tallied the number of interactions between partners over the course of their relationship.[6] Interestingly, the highest levels of communication were found at two points in the relationship: on the second date and during the last year of a failing marriage. On the second date, when things are beginning to look interesting, a man and woman want to find out everything about each other: questions fly back and forth, like, "What sort of movies do you like?" "Do you have any brothers and sisters?" "Where are you planning to work after you graduate?" And the final year before a separation is frequently riddled with recriminations: "If you had half as much interest in me as you had in your damned career, we could have had something!" "I'm sorry, but going over to your mama's house every evening is not my idea of a good time." A high level of communication may signal that changes are happening in a relationship, but it does not guarantee the quality of a relationship.

As a psychologist, I still cling to a belief in the magic of personal communication; open conversation does clear up commonplace misunderstandings that would otherwise stew into mistrust and resentment. And special moments of personal sharing carry heartfelt warmth that is to be cherished forever.

But communication is a two-edged sword that cuts both ways. To understand close personal communication, we must grapple with its darker qualities as well as its brighter and more supportive ones.

The good communication that builds a marriage does not merely mean clarity or honesty or completeness of messages. To the contrary, a great deal rides on the aim and intent behind what you say—on what is on your mind and in your heart. Consider this as we look at some common miscommunications between Paula, who wants more intimacy in her marriage, and Don, who seems to flee from it.

Progressing Apart

Unfortunately, intimate communication can solidify existing differences as easily as it can bridge them, and can thereby create less intimacy rather than more.

Don was not always so quiet around Paula. When they were first dating, many years back, he was in fact unusually outgoing with her. He always had friends, although they were pal-around friends more than talk-about-your-personal-problems friends. Don and his friends talked about school, about baseball, about what they would do Friday night, and about girls. But when Don was troubled, such as once when he got jilted, he kept it to himself. Pal-around friends do not pry.

But with Paula, he felt that he could talk about almost anything. Maybe he put his best foot forward and, as anyone might do, held a few things back that did not show him at his best. Paula was unusually understanding. In addition to his sweetheart, he considered her his closest friend. He was always respectful of her, if not particularly romantic. Paula thought him conscientious and figured he would make a good husband.

It was some time after they were married that things seemed to change. He came to look on marriage as an additional responsibility, as many men do, and he was consumed by it. Where he had always previously *wanted* to be with Paula, he now felt that he was deeply *obligated* to do so. His wanting and his attraction to her were gradually replaced by his sense of social, moral, and financial responsibility. And he began to resent her for making him feel so obligated.

Marriage provides couples with an inordinate amount of free time together that they did not have when they were living separately. The unprepared can quickly run out of things to say to each other, and Don was indeed unprepared. He now finds himself running out of things to say, and he wants time by himself—time away from the requirement to be the husband who must say something to or do something with the wife.

But Paula is in this marriage for the companionship, so something important is missing now that Don is no longer so interested in spending time with her. "Is anything wrong?" she asks him. "Nothing is wrong," he assures her—which hardly reassures her at all. She feels shut out. Obviously something is wrong or he would be more open with her. She becomes upset with him, telling herself he *ought* to be more involved, and she feels cheated. And she makes sure he knows it.

"I feel you take me for granted," she contends sometime later, and she pushes the point home. "I cook, I clean, I make everything easy for you. Is that what you want me for? A housekeeper and upstairs maid?"

"No. Really," he replies. Then there is silence. That was obviously not a strong answer, but what can he say? He feels sufficiently obligated as it is, and now he is hearing that what he does is not enough. She wants more from him. Not knowing what to say, but not wanting to make matters worse, he remains silent. He works to stay calm and waits for her to get over it.

Don could have said what she wanted him to say: "I do love you, really. You mean everything to me." An "I love you" would seem so simple to say, and it would have meant a great deal to Paula. Open expressions of love are perhaps the most obvious factor that women in happy marriages report having more than women in unhappy marriages.[7] But Don does not say it for a typically male reason that he himself does not understand much more than she does.

But this is important, and Paula persists. She asks the usual questions, and asks them again, but they remain unanswered. What does he feel? Why doesn't he talk to her more? Does he really love her? Why doesn't he show it? He looks for the right answer, but nothing he says is sufficient. Because he seems to be withholding, she feels justified in pressing him further for answers. By now, he is at a loss for what to say. He feels as if he were caught behind the lines and is being interrogated for important information that he does not possess. Within himself, he is quietly trying to figure out how to get away from her.

But by now, Paula is not simply hurt and upset over being ignored. She is angry about it as well. And her anger creeps into her voice as tears mix with coldness and accusation.

Actually, it is not women's tears by themselves that many men are unprepared to face; it is the combination of tears and anger. Had Paula been upset and crying but warm toward him, and had she asked for his support, Don could have tried to comfort her. He might have felt awkward about it, but he would have been willing to stay by her and hold her and talk to her. But along with her tears, he faces her accusations as well. He does not want to fight with her because she is obviously hurt and upset, but neither is he willing to comfort her in the face of her cold accusations. Moreover, any admission that he himself feels hurt by her would show weakness on his part, which would be unbecoming if not absolutely unmanly. Caught in the bind, he retreats further into his sanctuary of silence. And she continues to follow him there, to probe, to try to force him to open up and be with her.

Don is not apt to mention being confused by all this, and Paula does not look carefully enough to figure it out on her own. She sees only that he is silent, and she concludes that he does not understand how upset she is or that he does not care. And she feels even more injured because he does not seem to understand her feelings. So she goes to still greater lengths to force him to listen to her. She argues that he does not understand her and that he does not know how she feels.

Of course, he figures that he does understand her. He hears what she is saying, he recognizes that she is upset and angry at him, and he knows why. He is just disinclined to do what she wants, especially now. And he thinks it unfair of her to accuse him of not understanding. But how can he argue against her when she is the best judge of her own feelings? So he remains silent.

Such conversations are hardships for pursuers, who want more intimacy, and for distancers, who want less. They are hardships for pursuers because their quarry eludes them; and they are hardships for distancers because they cannot get away.

"Honey, we really have to talk about our relationship" surely sounds like an innocent opener. But to a wife pressing for more intimacy, it is the beginning of another round of frustrating pursuit. To her quiet and passive husband, it signals another round of intimate persecution.

Pursuers and distancers have their own identifiable activities. Pursuers ask for more involvement, complain about not having enough involvement, and become upset and even cold and critical when the companionship they seek is not forthcoming. One pursuing wife followed her husband around the house and into the bathroom, complaining all the while that he does not consider her feelings, seemingly oblivious to his wish to have some space to himself.

Distancers remain passive and withdrawn in the face of demands for more intimacy. They escape conveniently into the long hours of the workaholic, the obsession of the sports fanatic, the mindless comfort of the couch potato, or the welcome numbness of the alcoholic.

The attitudes of both are understandable and contribute predictably to each other's actions. As the husband withdraws, the wife feels neglected, hurt, and angry, and she pressures him for more involvement. And in response to her distress and accusation, he finds her impossible to contend with and withdraws further into himself. The pattern perpetuates itself (figure 4–1).

Once we understand this pattern, we can consider some proposals for more amicable involvement.

Love amid the Differences

How can those who want more involvement and those who want less find love and understanding amid their differences? Some married people conclude that differences in desired levels of

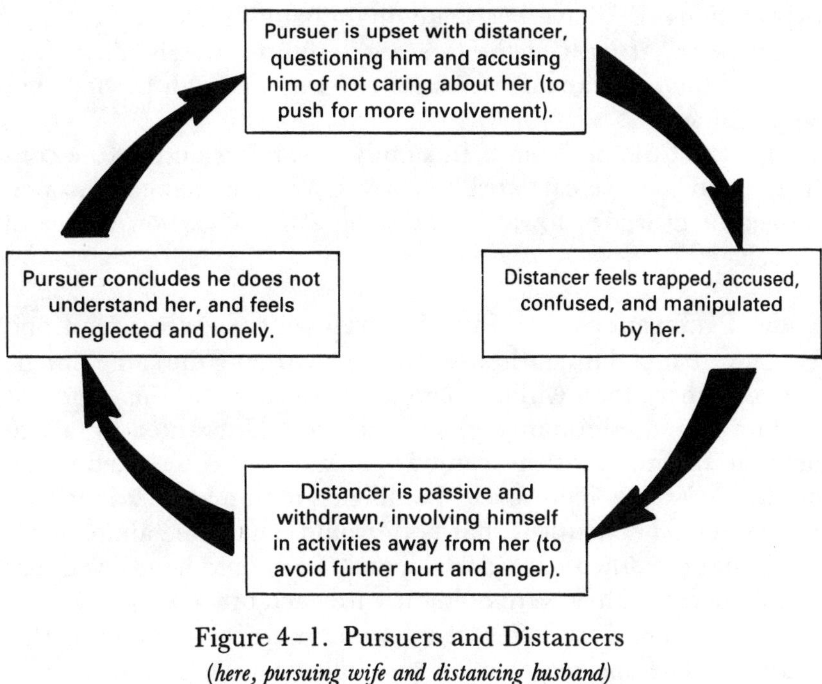

Figure 4–1. Pursuers and Distancers
(here, pursuing wife and distancing husband)

involvement are so ingrained between the sexes that they are unresolvable—that it is impossible to be happy with a mate so opposite from themselves.

But we would do well to distinguish between those differences that are ingrained, as opposed to the problems that arise from our responses to those differences. Many differences in preferred activities, in attitudes toward relationships, and in ways of communicating seem to be typical. Should we expect these to change? Is Don going to lose interest in watching sports or the thrill he feels out in the fresh air speeding along on his motorcycle? Is Paula going to find a new interest in bikes or in shooting pool and drinking beer with the boys? Who can say for sure? But under normal circumstances, probably not. Will Don acquire an interest in long conversations, admitting his vulnerabilities, and talking openly about love and other sensitive feelings? Proposals that men make such changes have been made over the last several decades, raising expectations that have been only marginally fulfilled by changes in behavior. At least in the foreseeable future, we should expect many of the familiar differences to remain, although perhaps not so prominently.

Much of the problem is in simply misunderstanding the contrasts, and that we can work to correct. We can change our often intolerant attitudes toward those who are not carbon copies of ourselves.

Some Preferences Are Simply Preferences. When Don and Paula were first dating, they seemed to love doing the same things. Don was more than willing to go to the theater with her, and out to dinner, and even dancing now and then. He wanted to talk to her almost as much as she wanted to talk to him. Paula liked riding on the back of his motorcycle, holding on to him as he leaned into the corners. The truth is that both would have done almost anything that the other wanted to do, and they would have loved it—simply because they were doing it with each other.

Then, sometime after they were married, much of this changed. The specific activity gradually took on greater importance than just being with each other. So Don no longer wants to go out to dinner with Paula, which she interprets to mean that he no longer loves her. But it is not that he no longer wants to be around her. He would love for her to ride the bike with him again, but she now thinks that bike riding is too dangerous. He would love for her to watch television with him, but she now feels it is a waste of time.

Paula is misunderstanding the problem and taking it personally. The problem is not that he no longer loves her; he simply wants to do what he likes to do, while she wants him to do with her what she wants to do. Each wants the other to share his or her preferences.

All this is merely the normal process of settling into a relationship. When love is new, couples may not care much what they do, as long as they do it together. But when they settle in together, their individual preferences reassert themselves.

So while Paula wants Don to prefer having conversations to riding bikes, she should not take it so personally that he does not. He simply prefers to ride. She need not conclude that his love for her is gone. Nor should he conclude that because she no longer wants to ride the bike, she has lost interest in him.

Perhaps we are all fooled, however slightly, by the romance of a courtship that so easily overrides our other preferences. But at the time, few of us really want to see past our fantasies.

The moral here is simple. If you and your mate prefer to do different things, try not to see it as a failure of love. Love has as much to do with respecting preferences as with remaking them to match your own. And remember that many preferences are only that—just preferences. It is how we respond to each other's preferences that is crucial.

How Do You Say "Love"? If tender words are used to convey love, their absence seems to reveal an absence of love. But this is not always the case, because many men and women miscommunicate about the meaning of love.

A straightforward "I love you" seems so simple to say. Since so many women want to hear it, why do so many men have trouble saying it? "Do you really love me?" is a common question women ask. "I mean, seriously–do you?"

A man of few words and little tact gives the briefest of answers: "I'm here, aren't I?" That is his answer—take it or leave it. Perhaps he truly feels he answered the question. Obviously, his wife is outraged.

Paula asks the same question of Don, and he wrestles with what it means to love and tries to be honest with himself in his answer. He says it more tactfully, but his basic message is about the same: "I know I want to be married to you. I am satisfied to go to work every morning, because I know that I am supporting you and that you are there for me. I would never want to leave you, and I would never want you to leave me. Is that what you mean by love?"

This answer leaves her unsatisfied. "But why can't you say you *love* me?"

Why, indeed! But Don did in fact say he loved her, in his own words rather than in her words. Paula did not grasp this. She thinks of love as a feeling one might or might not experience, and he thinks of it as a commitment to being with a woman and working to provide for her. This is one of the differences between how men and women tend to think about relationships.

Many men do not say the words "I love you" simply because they do not think in those terms. But they do say "I love you" in their own terms—in terms of their commitment to building a life together.

Two teenagers who were going steady asked exactly the opposite questions about each other. "Why can't he say he loves me?" the girl asked, especially puzzled because her boyfriend did seem to want only her and did not look at other girls. She wanted to experience more of the excitement of love before she settled down. But he asked, "How can she say she loves me and then be flirting with other guys all over school the next day?" She did not think there was anything wrong with a little flirting, especially since he had not even said he loved her. These two were talking past each other, as men and women so often do.

There is a difference between *feeling* love and *meaning* it.[8] Women may view love more as a romantic feeling, and when that feeling is gone, the experience is over for them. Men may tend to view love as more of a commitment, so that expressing love is promising to be true. This difference appears early, even among teenagers. Girls talk about love easily because they feel it, whereas boys are reluctant to say the words because they are not sure they mean it—and do not want to pledge that sort of commitment. So it is not surprising the two misunderstand each other. Interestingly, after some experience with this, many women avoid talking too quickly about love for fear of scaring a man off. They learn to understand that talking about love implies making a commitment, which may send him fleeing for his freedom.

Other reasons for the difference have been proposed as well. One is that men don't say "I love you" because it sounds stupid to them. After it has been said once, these gents argue, there's no reason to repeat it over and over like a trained seal yapping on cue from a handler. Some of them resent being expected to mouth words that are not the ones they themselves would choose to reflect their views. I suspect that for many men, acknowledging love also implies exposing a vulnerability—it is admitting that they have a weakness for someone who is important enough to have considerable control over their feelings. So many men may avoid talking about love because it implies they lack self-sufficiency.

Listen for Love. What does all this suggest for better communication? What should women who want more romantic communication in the marriage do? My main conclusion is that they should listen more carefully to what their husbands say in their own language, then translate it into the words of their choice. To most men, making a willing commitment to a life together counts as love. So if your husband answers in those terms, translate it as love in your terms. And appreciate the meaning behind it.

There is an old saying that good communication depends not on how much you say but on how well you hear. Those who seek more intimacy are well advised to become better listeners. By reflecting back what you hear to your partner, you can improve your listening. If you hear that he feels the commitment itself is important, let him know that you hear it. A simple "I hear you saying that you are willing to make a life with me" should do nicely.

Men too would do well to understand these different languages and to translate. When your wife wants reassurance that you love her, you need not draw a mental blank and retreat into silence. You can talk about what the marriage means to you in terms that you understand. Then work to bridge the language gap so that she will understand what goes on in your mind.

Aside from being wonderful, words of love can also be a lot of trouble. Some individuals could be more careful with them, so that they serve as genuine tokens of affection and not as banners in an ongoing joust over who is and who is not sufficiently intimate.

Why Ask "Why?" "Why won't you say you love me?" "Why can't you talk to me?" "Why don't you want to be with me?" In some marriages, these questions become the substance of many conversations, and no answer seems to quite satisfy. If you find yourself asking your mate why and why again, and then again, you might ask *yourself* why.

Obviously, you ask a question to get an answer. You want information so you can try to understand. You listen to what someone says and mull it over. You arrive at your conclusions and therefore are better informed.

But when you get an answer that you do not want, you may continue asking the question anyway. You do not want just any answer—you are after the particular answer you want to hear. And you are none the wiser for persisting. "Why?" is an inquiry, but it can also be a complaint. People often ask "why?" when they do not *like* what someone is doing, in a voice that says that they object: "Why won't you say you love me?" If you ask this more than once, you are probably pushing your man to recognize that he has no valid reason *not* to say it and that therefore that he *should* say it. He answers that he has already said it, but that is not what you wanted to hear, and so you ask again. You are ignoring his answer and trying to provoke the answer you want.

If you feel you do not understand why your mate acts the way he or she does, ask yourself what it is that you really want. Do you just want to comprehend, or do you want a change? If you want to comprehend, do go ahead and ask why. But if what you really want is a change, you would do better to request the change that you want.

Who Does Not Understand? If you frequently complain that your man does not understand, you should realize that communication can become slippery, because *understand* has two separate meanings. *To understand* means "to see," "to hear," "to recognize," "to comprehend," or "to grasp with the intellect." But *to understand* also means "to tolerate," "to make allowances," "to be supportive," or "to be understanding toward someone."

Your complaint that your man does not understand you is likely to cause confusion rather than comprehension. He probably does understand, in the sense that he knows you are upset; but he does *not* understand, in the sense that he is not sympathetic and supportive. When the problem is that he is not supportive, it is better to state that directly than to say that he does not understand. "I think you may know how I feel," you might say, "but I want you to be more supportive of what I am going through." Your man may or may not follow your request to be more supportive, but either way, you will both understand better what is going on.

Intimacy Must Be Nurtured. It is one thing to *expect* warmth and communication as a right and then to be justifiably upset and angry when it is not there. It is another thing to actually *cultivate* intimacy, carefully and by plan. It is those who choose the latter course who remain cozy with each other over years of marriage.

Pursuers who respond with hurt and anger to a lack of intimacy are apt to invite cautious aloofness in their mates, which provokes further hurt and anger. If you find yourself upset when closeness is missing, look at your own reactions. Consider whether your own attitude is driving your mate farther away from you. As a general rule, women's combination of hurt and anger affects men much more strongly than they allow women to see. If you are unsure, get a second opinion. Ask the one closest to the situation—your husband.

Saying you are upset sometimes means you are actually angry as well. It is common to be both upset and angry over the same thing. Being ignored is both upsetting, because the warmth is missing, and a source of anger, because it seems that someone is withholding warmth. But while upset and anger often go together naturally, it is important to learn to separate them. Men who are reluctant to be open will close down further in the face of these two emotions together.

A message given warmly is more likely to be received than one given with a snarl. If you miss the closeness, try to talk about it without anger. Many men are so used to hearing accusation with women's tears that they cannot separate the two. They conclude that a woman who cries must be condemning them for hurting her so, or at least for not fixing whatever is wrong.

When you are sad, you can usually ask your husband for comfort *as long as you are warm about it.* You might want to say clearly that you are just troubled, making it clear that it is not his fault. You could even mention that it is comforting just that he is there with you.

Many husbands—even those who do not seem particularly affectionate—do very well when asked for something specific. Say specifically what you want from him, being sure that it is something that he actually can do. And whatever he does, even the smallest beginning, appreciate it. Simple words work magic: "Just sit here with me for a while." "Sometimes I really miss you." "It really helps when you are here listening to me like this." Men tend to feel uncommonly useful when their presence is regarded as a benefit rather than as a liability, and will be willing to repeat the experience.

Suppose you suggest having a talk about your relationship. Your husband gives you that "Oh no, here we go again" expression and glances around for the nearest exit. Obviously, it is natural for you to be exasperated, but instead, try to hear what he feels. You yourself recognize that these conversations have often wound into lengthy arguments in the past.

"You're not looking forward to this," you suggest. Your voice stays warm.

"Well, no," he answers.

"Afraid I'm going to be cross with you?"

"I guess I just never know what to say."

Of course he suspects that you will become annoyed with him, if that has been your pattern. Answer his implicit concern: "I am not annoyed or anything. I just have some things I need to talk about."

A conversation that begins this way is off to a good start. Women who provide the warmth and guidance in such conversations usually find that their otherwise silent husbands are quite willing to continue.

Husbands who miss intimacy would do well to control their annoyance and to show their softer feelings. Men who feel taken for granted are apt to criticize or sulk rather than admit that they are lonely. When men feel insecure or sad, it is better for them to muster their courage and talk to their wives about it.

Surely someone has suggested this before. The too-typical husband who withdraws from such conversations should recognize by now that he is inviting further pursuit. The wife who wants to be heard does not simply vanish because he does not wish to listen. Before the marriage, were he to vanish, she would probably get the message in good time and go her own way as well. After marriage, as long as she wants an intimate relationship with you and not an affair, you are all she has available. The conversation you walked away from today will still be waiting for you tomorrow.

Husbands who distance themselves might look more closely at why they do so. Is your wife so hard to talk to? Are you perhaps confused or intimidated by her seemingly relentless questions or by her moodiness? How much of your withdrawal is actually a power tactic, to show her that she cannot get away with making too many demands? Is it a way of saying "Don't mess with me, or you won't see me"?

Answering these questions requires some thought. If you are somewhat intimidated by her, brave your lapse in manly posturing and tell her about it: "When you're upset at me, I get tense inside. You're better at arguing than I am, so you usually have the last word. But whenever I say something you don't like, you get really hurt, and then I feel terrible."

But if your withdrawal is also a power tactic, be careful! You can indeed make a tough statement by withdrawing from your wife. But this is likely merely to perpetuate the problems. She will pursue you to show that you cannot get away with it. Surely there are better ways to communicate!

The routine strains between pursuers and distancers can be resolved not necessarily by more communication or less, but by *better* communication. Pursuers might talk a little less, allowing more room to breathe, and it would surely help if distancers would talk more. But both would do well to listen more carefully and to genuinely try to understand each other.

5

Givers and Takers

Most of us expect that our contributions to a marriage should be balanced, at least approximately, by what we gain in return. When our benefits compensate for our sacrifices, we are likely to be satisfied with the arrangement. Research confirms this commonsense notion, finding that those who feel that there is a fair and equitable balance between the give and the take are apt to be happier with their marriages than those who do not.[1]

Husband and wife need not contribute the *same* things for the marriage to feel fair to both. One might provide the income, while the other raises the children and arranges the social calendar; one might be joyful but impulsive, while the other is patient and responsible, so that they complement each other. But whatever the particulars, an equitable arrangement is more likely to produce contentment and long-term stability.

But not all stable relationships appear to involve approximately equal contributions between the two partners. Some look imbalanced, lopsided, and unfair, with one partner doing all the giving and the other doing little but taking. The hardworking wife with a ne'er-do-well husband holds the family together and never complains, while their close friends conclude that she is too good for him and ought to leave him. A husband earns the living and returns home to provide emotional support for his unhappy wife, while she has nothing better to do than complain that he does not understand how she feels.

Some givers-and-takers relationships do fail, but others continue over many years and in spite of the puzzling imbalances. These fascinating entanglements often appear to simply ignore the fairness principle. In this pattern, it is the very *imbalance* between husband and wife that provides unexpected stability.

The Match. Most of us want to contribute to a partnership and to be sustained by it in return—both to give and to take. But a few individuals are primarily givers or primarily takers in many of their important relationships. *Givers* are those who feel compelled to caretake for others and are unwilling to be taken care of in return. Always concerned about others, they are generous to a fault. *Takers* expect a free ride or at least an easy one, and they seldom consider those around them. Always concerned about themselves, they are selfish and egotistical and sometimes lazy as well.

Givers and takers sort through the sea of acquaintances and manage to find each other, for the obvious reason.[2] One is looking for a foundling to nurture, and the other is looking for help in the struggles of life. And if and when one such pairing fails, some of these sturdy adventurers find a similar match once again. It is not only in folklore that an individual breaks free of a marriage with an alcoholic, only to marry another alcoholic just falling off the wagon.

"I was important to him," mentioned one woman in trying to explain why she had married an alcoholic for the second time. Freely translated, she is saying simply, "He had a deep need that I felt I could fulfill." The caretaking men who marry needy women give much the same explanation: "I was important to her" or "She was so vulnerable, and I really wanted to take care of her."

Thoroughbred givers are not likely to pair with other givers. If a woman who always gives and cannot receive goes out with a fellow who is the same way, each tries to give but nothing is ever gracefully accepted. Neither feels appreciated for what he or she could contribute, and the relationship is awkward and frustrating.

Givers. Givers are always concerned about pleasing, but not merely because they find it pleasing to do so. Givers feel strongly obligated to look after those they love, and they are trying to fulfill their responsibilities. As perplexing as it seems, givers' primary concern is that they are not doing enough for those close to them. When things do go wrong, they are quick to blame themselves for it. "I could have done more to help him!" the giver supposes.

"Perhaps she would not be so moody if I had been stronger and more cheerful around her." Givers also worry about being selfish: "If only I could have done more and not thought of myself so much!" Burdened already by the pain of those around them, they blame themselves for failing to make it better.

When her temperamental husband loses yet another job, an overly responsible wife cannot stand to see him in such pain and worries that she has somehow failed him. She takes it upon herself to maintain the household, to allow him however much time he needs to pull himself back together. So does an overly responsible husband, whose wife is unusually touchy and never satisfied. He feels he has failed her and tries to make it up to her.

It is their pervasive sense of obligation that makes givers unable to receive. While they may also fear that being nurtured implies that they are weak, their reluctance to receive goes deeper than that. Burdened already in their social relations, givers feel that accepting anything more from people would increase their debt to them. Some reciprocity is usually expected in families, but givers are especially frightened about owing anyone anything. Overwhelmed already by what they feel they owe, givers do not want more burdens. So givers cannot take out of fear of acquiring further obligations.

Many givers recall that as children they felt responsible for taking care of their own mothers or fathers, and felt selfish or guilty whenever they received anything special for themselves. Some recall that Mom or Dad frequently made them feel selfish or guilty for wanting anything at all for themselves. Whatever was given to them had a string attached that said they owed something in return. Used to being manipulated by what appeared to be love, as adults they cannot accept love that is given freely, with no strings attached.

Contrary to what one might expect, givers are not particularly angry. Giving continually and receiving little would grate quickly on most people, but committed givers feel that they are the ones who are giving too little and not fulfilling their responsibilities, regardless of how it appears to outsiders. So they feel inadequate and guilty over their failings rather than angry. It is not that they suppress their anger, although givers are uncomfortable with anger and try to keep the peace. It is that as the "responsible" parties, they see no one to blame but themselves.

When givers do become angry, they begin to limit their giving. Their anger pushes them to challenge and confront rather than give in to the demands others place on them. When givers begin to feel cheated, they gear up to demand something in return.

Takers. Takers are trying to satisfy themselves, and they see nothing wrong with that. It is not that they mean to be unfair, and they surely do not see themselves as unprincipled or selfish. It is simply that the world is itself competitive and unprincipled, and nothing is given freely. Takers see that they must reach and grab for themselves merely to get their fair share in life. And yet whatever they do get in life falls far short of what they feel they have a right to expect. Takers feel cheated out of their rightful share of the good things in life.

Takers' philosophy is that life should be easier for them than it is. When faced with hardship and disappointments, they are little inclined to work harder or to become more tolerant. Takers resent the unfairness, they sulk and complain, they blame those around them, and they demand more.

Life is especially rough for takers when those close to them seem better off than they are themselves. After quitting what he considered to be a nowhere job, an unemployed man listened to his stubbornly cheerful wife explain how she could support the family while he found something that he really wanted to do. It seemed bitterly unfair to him that she should have a good job she liked while he had nothing. "She acts like I'm invisible," he complained, angry that he was no longer receiving the respect due him. Similarly, a wife who has the free time to do whatever she wishes might resent her husband because he goes to a job that makes him feel important.

Takers are little inclined to appreciate their caregiving partners or to see that they are getting more than their fair share. If they did, they would feel pressured to contribute more themselves. Rather than face their shortcomings, takers try to turn the tables. "She never gives anything willingly," one taker complained again and again, somewhat typically. Since she gave nothing willingly, he implied, she deserved no credit for what she did contribute. And he did not need to feel squeezed to give anything in return.

Takers may have grown up with parents who were overly indulgent and required little of them in return. Some recall being neglected but being given what they wanted when they fussed and complained, which they learned to do to get what they want. Some were bought off with material possessions to compensate for the shortage of parental time and affection. So they learned to look out for themselves and to not be too concerned with those around them.

The Mix

Givers and takers interact with each other to maintain their already imbalanced inclinations. Tom, a self-indulgent fellow accustomed to getting whatever he wants, is married to a generous wife, Gail, who is cheerful herself and bound and determined to keep everyone else happy at any cost. Tom, an inveterate consumer with expensive hobbies, has a motorcycle and a sports car, which he races. Subject to frequent periods of moodiness, he feels that he is not really getting what he wants and that life is not as good to him as it ought to be. He works, although he has quit several jobs when he found them tedious and unfulfilling.

Gail also feels that life should be better for him than it is. She had originally supported buying the motorcycle, which she felt would be a good outlet for his frustrations. When the weather turned cold and he tired of riding the bike, she supported buying the sports car. She attended many rallies with him, providing companionship and cheering him on.

But the initial excitement faded, and the rallies became routine. Tom again found himself at loose ends and argued that they should purchase a lake house an hour out of town. Gail opposed this because of the long commute and the isolation from her friends that it would mean. But since he needed somewhere to be happy, she gave in. The lake was an ideal place for a small yacht, which he soon purchased, and then the yacht obviously needed a dock, which he leased at the nearby marina.

Gail, the family's money manager, finally complained that they could not afford so many additional expenses. But Tom angrily accused her of trying to take away the few things that gave him some joy in life. Concerned that she was causing him pain, she conceded once again and hoped for the best.

The long commute to and from the lake house took its toll on the relationship, leaving fewer hours for them to be together. When she spent more time with the children and her friends than with him, he felt neglected and unwanted. When she asked him to clean up the living room or do the dishes, he felt belittled and nagged, and he snarled at her that she was impossible and cared more about cleaning the house than about him.

Gail still wants to make his life wonderful for him but now worries that she is not doing enough. Since he is tired, she blames herself for not managing to get the house picked up without bothering him about it. Getting angry at him would only make things worse, she knows, so it is not really an option. He is injured and fragile, after all, and any anger she casts his way might push him so far that he finally leaves her—or perhaps purchases a small private airplane. Recognizing that she would lose any confrontation, she concedes quickly, and maintains the peace. She takes on still more of the responsibilities and searches for ways to better manage them.

Gail considered leaving the marriage once or twice, but she always rejected that option because she felt that there was something more that she could have done or should do now to make it better. She remembers some of their early times together, when he seemed to really appreciate her, and she wants those same feelings back again.

Through the Eyes of Their Mates. Givers see themselves through the eyes of those they want to please. Inclined to feel responsible, they literally soak up every word or innuendo of blame that is cast their way. Takers have a way of making those close to them feel responsible for their lives, and givers are very inclined to accept that responsibility. When an intermittent alcoholic is hurt and upset by something his wife says and goes on a binge, whose responsibility is it? Regardless of who caused the incident, the responsibility for managing things while he is intoxicated falls on his wife and on the rest of the family. So in this limited sense, she is "responsible." Rightfully concerned, she is careful to avoid doing anything that might annoy him and cause another unpleasant incident.

Givers are unwilling to see takers for what they are. Generous by nature and unwilling to condemn, they are reluctant to draw the harsh conclusion that their husband or wife is narcissistic and selfish. They make allowances, find excuses, consider the circumstances, or just ignore the vast accumulation of signs that all point to the same conclusion. For example, Gail feels that her overspending husband loves her but is just going through some rough times. She will not admit that Tom is more concerned with his own hobbies than with her or the family. By the same token, the considerate wife of an alcoholic might tell herself that her unconscious husband really does love her and the children but that the alcohol makes him unable to show it. She would not say that he chooses alcohol over the family and has done so for so long that he barely recognizes his family anymore. The truly considerate husband says that his angry wife loves him but is just having a hard time with life. Any implication that the mate is being inconsiderate would just cause a fight, so it is better to not even think that way.

Since givers are basically protective of their mates, they seldom complain about their marriages, even to their family or to their closest friends. So givers are not swamped with outside opinions on how unusual their marriages really are, and they do not receive the support that might help them stand up for themselves.

Privileged Characters. Why is Tom not more appreciative of all the allowances Gail makes for his preferences? A tangle of cobwebs lies in the taker's mentality. Takers are often appreciative in the beginning but quickly turn sour. Acting like a privileged character, Tom takes what he has for granted and then expects more. Gail feels she ought to do more for him, and he agrees with her fully. He too sees himself through the eyes of his partner. His unfulfilled expectations trigger anger and accusation, and he complains continually in order to push her to further concessions. Unfortunately, he believes his own complaints, focusing only on what is missing and overlooking the satisfactions that might otherwise be his. Little concerned about those around him, he feels isolated in the narrow pursuit of his own selfish interests.

Takers are oblivious to the hardships they create for those they supposedly love. A balanced view of their contributions would overwhelm them, and they are not inclined anyway to face themselves honestly. By blaming their caretakers, they avoid taking responsibility for themselves.

No Monopolies by Gender. Similar issucs play out between giving men and taking women. When one unusually considerate man comes home to find his moody wife worn out from her afternoon of soap operas and game shows, he cannot confront her with the fact that the house is a wreck and that there are no plans for supper. Since his wife is depressed and barely holding on anyway, he feels it would be unwise to mention these small problems. She would only get angry at him, as she has done before, stomp into her room, and stay there until he apologizes and coaxes her back out. So he cleans up the place himself, cooks or takes her out to dinner and arranges to have friends over whom he feels she will enjoy. And he chooses his words carefully, avoiding any accusation lest he upset her further. Touchy individuals who are at loose ends with themselves can be tyrants over partners who try to maintain the peace and make sure the ordinary things get done. And because givers are so self-sufficient, takers feel even more unappreciated and useless.

Since their giving mates could get a better deal in another relationship, takers are touchy about the possibility that they might be abandoned. Were a caretaking husband to recognize that he does it all and gets nothing in return, he might leave. So his wife accuses him of being insensitive and selfish, which serves to shake his confidence and to obligate him to stay.

Givers and takers are opposites in many ways, but they agree on who is responsible. When things go wrong, givers feel that they have not given enough, and takers feel that they are being cheated by the emptiness of their marriages.

Givers Produce Takers. Not all giver-and-taker relationships begin that way. Many such couples appear evenly matched when they marry, but then seemingly minor imbalances between them build. Givers try to make life a little too soft and easy for their partners, expecting little or nothing in return. And as we all know, it is easy to do nothing in circumstances where nothing is expected of us. By shouldering the burdens too willingly, givers create a taker mentality in what would otherwise be fair-minded and helpful partners.

A nurturant woman who is outwardly calm and supportive when her husband quits his job recognizes that it is a difficult time and wants to avoid pressuring him. But in so doing, she risks maintaining the status quo. By her very sturdiness, she conveys that she is so strong that she does not really need him—that she can easily manage all by herself. So he does not see the strain he is placing on her, and he does not experience the panic and the burdens that she experiences. Were he to see her fears and the upcoming hardships, he might feel more pressure to look for work, and more important, to protect and provide for her. By being too generous, she prevents him from experiencing a normal sense of responsibility that he should feel for his wife and family.

The same conclusion applies to the responsible man who is too proud to tell his wife that he cannot manage the bills on his own and needs her to help. He adds the overtime and the additional night job too willingly and without comment. She complains that he is gone too much and cannot see how hard it really is on him. Were he to show her the pain of his solitary and weary existence, she might be more than willing to do whatever she could to help. But by accepting his extra load too easily, he invites her to take what he does do for granted and to attend only to what he fails to do. Men who avoid showing any vulnerability or weakness pose particular problems for their wives, who feel unneeded and so turn their attention elsewhere.

So by their attitudes and their actions, givers and takers invite and then support complementary attitudes in each other. Givers feel that they have not done enough, and so they do it all and make allowances for their partners. Takers feel cheated and unimportant, and so they accuse their partners for doing too little to help them out. The pattern perpetuates itself (figure 5–1).

Overdoers and Slackers. Overdoers are like givers in that they overfunction in the family, doing much more than their share of the work.[3] But where givers act out of sympathy and concern, overdoers have other motivations. Overdoers want to control all

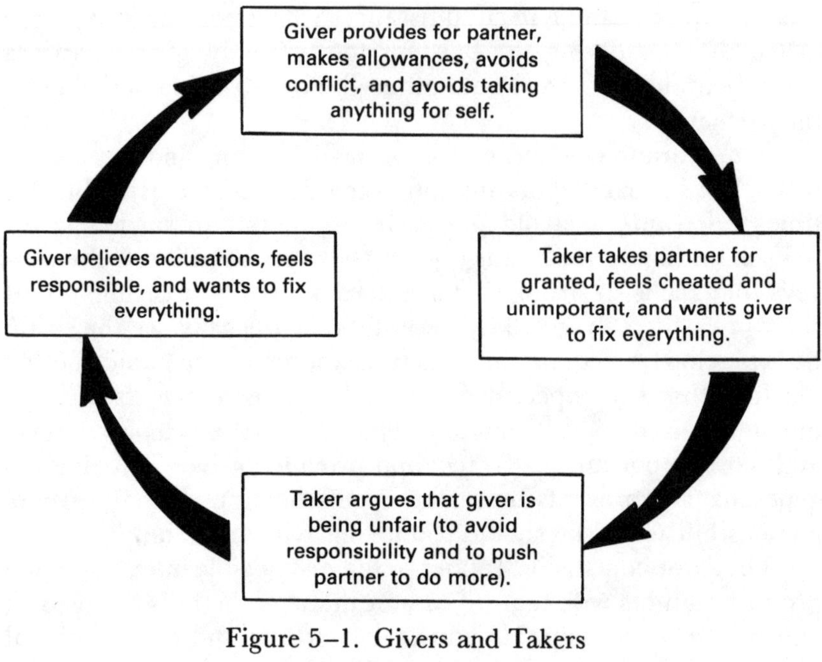

Figure 5–1. Givers and Takers

aspects of their marriages, to be the important one. They take charge of the ordinary household tasks not to make life easier on their partners, but because it is satisfying for them to be in charge.

An overdoer wife complains that her husband does not do the dishes or much of anything else to help around the house. But when he begins to do the job, she snaps at him for not rinsing them sufficiently before loading them into the dishwasher and for placing them on the wrong racks. Individuals do have their own preferences for how to load a dishwasher, but this woman is not merely suggesting that he do it a particular way and guiding him in his trial run. By barking at him, she makes him feel inadequate and ensures that he will allow her to load the dishwasher as she wishes. She conveys that she is truly indispensable, for nothing would be done properly without her. Finding it impossible to please her, he takes the path of least resistance, stops trying, ducks out of all the household tasks, and tries to stay out of the way.

Overdoers feel important, because nothing would go right without them, but they also feel worried and burdened, because nothing would go right without them. Overdoers are frequently annoyed at having to do so much themselves and feel taken for granted and unappreciated. Apparently, they overlook the obvious—that it is their own insistence on doing it all (or at least supervising) that invites their partners to do so little. Overdoers simply move in and take over, then resent doing it all while their partners do next to nothing. It is this attitude of annoyance that separates overdoers from the standard givers, who accept their lots more pleasantly.

Givers who grow tired from their one-way bargains can easily become overdoers. Too many frustrations and too little appreciation can burn out their compassion and concern for their taking partners. The warmth and special connection of the early relationship is lost, and they begin to feel taken for granted and cheated out of the fulfillment that should accompany marriage. Givers who become so worn out that they turn angry and gripe and complain are on their way to looking out for themselves (unless they come to feel guilty about that, too, and try to make amends). Surely better resolutions are available for givers and takers in these patterns.

Rebalancing the Give-and-Take

Perhaps the most perplexing snafu in giver-and-taker relationships is that neither the giver nor the taker seems to understand which is which. Givers and takers must properly identify themselves as a minimal beginning to planning changes. Realize as you read this that most of us have some combination of giving and taking characteristics, which is healthy, and that you need not identify yourself as strictly one or the other.

A Catch-22 for Not-So-Easy Identification. When givers and takers do try to identify themselves, more often than not they get it backward. Worried that they are being selfish and not doing enough to help, givers fear that they are actually takers. Takers, in turn, feel cheated, and see themselves as inveterate givers who must fight to receive their fair share of anything in return.

A catch-22 is a system that is just crazy enough to catch anyone who is sane enough to want to get out of it. In the novel *Catch-22,* by Joseph Heller, any airman who wanted out of the army-air corps in the midst of World War II was trapped.[4] He had to be certifiably insane to get out of the army, but the army itself was certifiably insane and so was anyone who wanted to serve in it. Since the ones who wanted out of it were the only really sane ones, their petitions for discharge on the grounds of mental instability were automatically denied, since their request for discharge was proof of their sanity. A catch-22 snares those who take the most logical route to escape.

If you always see yourself as a giver who receives too little in return, you are as likely to be a taker; but if you usually worry that you are a selfish taker and that you give too little of yourself, you are likely to be a giver. Whichever you are sure you are, chances are you are fooling yourself.

Fortunately, this catch-22 can be helpful if you realize that it provides only a mirror image, which you must then reverse. Those who worry that they are not doing enough and who feel selfish when they ask for anything are not takers, as they fear, and should probably identify themselves as givers. And those who feel cheated and often angry at how much they sacrifice are not really givers, as they assume, and should consider whether they are takers. Identify yourself here not by your justification but by what is in your heart. Are your concerns primarily for your partner or for yourself?

Identification is a stubborn problem, for givers are surprisingly reluctant to see themselves as givers or their mates as takers, while takers are reluctant to see themselves as takers (perhaps not so surprisingly). Assistance from an impartial counselor or an extraordinarily objective and forthright friend may be necessary.

In most marriages the give-and-take stays somewhat balanced. It is only in the most lopsided relationships that the partners are strictly givers and takers. Yet even in relatively equitable pairings, there may be periods in which one partner becomes mainly a giver and the other mainly a taker. Perhaps one partner tries to make too many allowances and the other takes advantage of it, at least until the situation changes and the imbalance is corrected. The majority of us who are not prototype givers or takers might nonetheless see some of ourselves in this pattern and try some of the following suggestions.

Givers Must Be Willing to Receive. If you are a giver, you must learn to expect more from your partner and take less on yourself. But reordering the give-and-take requires making some basic changes in attitudes.

Be More Realistic. Givers must make an accurate estimate of how much they actually contribute. If you view yourself through the eyes of an ungrateful housemate, you will readily see yourself as selfish and inadequate and basically unworthy. You must learn to claim for yourself a fair share of the credit. It is especially important to have friends with whom to share your experiences. A good listener can confirm your observations and provide some standards of what is and is not fair and normal in a marriage.

Givers could also use an advanced-noise-reduction filter to tune out the static of continuing accusations. See fast-and-loose accusations not as simple observations but as bold manipulations meant to force concessions. Arguing over such accusations produces only confusion and should be avoided. Remember, takers are *supposed* to complain—it is written into their job descriptions. The mate who genuinely appreciates what the giver does hardly qualifies as a real taker.

By Your Fruits Shall Ye Be Known. Since givers are so concerned about those they love, they might look more closely at what they achieve by their compulsory contributions. While they are trying to be helpful, having low expectations of their mates produces low achievements. The woman who allows her husband to spend all the family money on his own hobbies must realize that she is doing him no favor. Although she wants life to be easier for him, her acquiesence allows him to slide pleasantly into shallow and blithely irresponsible pastimes with little substance and few lasting satisfactions. Soon, when he becomes unhappy again, she must realize that doing more of the same cannot provide a more lasting solution. She must allow him to face the strains of life squarely so that he can begin to master them.

The man who busies himself trying to make life pleasant for his unhappy wife must also realize that whatever he does to ease the strains only makes her less able to face them herself. He must be willing to allow her to confront her own demons so that she can begin to gain control of them.

Givers can be unwitting enablers, as the support they provide enables those they love to continue in perhaps pleasant but ultimately harmful activities. Making the allowances that enable an alcoholic to continue drinking does him no favor. One who wants to give something meaningful must do more than ease the most immediate stressors and satisfy the itch. Gifts that bear fruit must have substance. Those who really love must be willing to insist on sharing the troubles and joys of mutual responsibility. Says the familiar James Dobson truism, love must be tough.[5]

Expect More of Your Fellow Adult. Givers must ask for help. The superwife who comes home from her job and goes on to tackle housework and homework must recognize her limits and rein in her ambitions. She must ask for help, but calmly and without annoyance. She might write a list of what has to be done that evening and invite her husband to choose what of it he wants to do.

If he declines her invitation and seems unwilling to do more, she must be willing to do less. If he does nothing to help clean up the house, it may be because his standards of cleanliness are slightly lower than hers. She becomes uncomfortable and does it all before he notices that anything needs doing. But if his shirts go unwashed for a week and meals are no longer served, chances are he will notice that something is amiss. Only when he himself is inconvenienced by the unwashed laundry might he be interested in doing a greater share of the work.

That is the point to begin to renegotiate the workload. But the giver must plan carefully and estimate how much chaos he or she can tolerate. Leaving the mess in the kitchen is probably a loser, for the mess is unlikely to bother the one who does not cook the meals. Amenities that are unimportant to the taking mate will simply be left undone. So givers should choose their battlegrounds and be patient. Old habits can be stubborn, and initial changes may be piecemeal and tentative.

Show Vulnerability. Givers appear so proficient at managing on their own that others simply take it for granted. Reluctant to show panic or inadequacy, givers feign confidence so that others can feel secure. Little wonder that their mates feel so little obligation to help out. The advice is obvious: When you are well over your head and struggling to stay afloat, say so! The woman whose husband spends their last nickel of credit need not look secure and confident. Better she should tell her husband she is scared of owing so much money and cannot handle it all by herself. And if her fears pressure him to be more supportive, so much the better.

Perhaps he should already have known that she was scared, but he may not have known at all. It is surprising how seldom takers consider the hardships they produce for those around them. Givers who admit they are overwhelmed and afraid may find that their mates respond in surprisingly supportive ways. Their weaker side may invite an understanding and protectiveness that never showed up as long as they concealed their vulnerabilities. Many supposed takers respond from the heart when it becomes obvious that someone really needs them. Those who simply resent the pressure, however, are ill prepared to change under any circumstances.

Takers Might Be More Appreciative. Takers can sound cold and unsympathetic, but these same qualities are shared by many others as well—only in smaller and more manageable proportions. Takers feel shortchanged and cheated in their marriages, which many others feel occasionally as well. Takers are simply more committed to the narrow pursuit of their own comforts and are quicker than most to lose patience with those who do not satisfy their expectations.

Our trendy culture, no longer so concerned with sacrifice and social contribution, now emphasizes loving yourself first and looking out for number one.[6] It does not advocate doing anyone harm, but the focus on self slides ambiguously into narcissism and greed. When people feel unhappy or unfulfilled, their obvious conclusion is that they are missing out and need a greater share to satisfy themselves. How much should you have to sacrifice, and how can any of us be sure that we are getting our fair share?

If happiness and fulfillment were indicators of the satisfaction of people's needs, then those who focus mainly on themselves would be more fulfilled and those who reach out to others would be unfulfilled. But it does not often work that way, as should be apparent enough to those who tally their experiences. Psychologist Erik Erikson included "generativity" along with intimacy on his list of critical life stages, arguing that contributing to family and community is essential to a fulfilling life.[7] It is those who commit themselves who can feel they belong to something greater and more permanent than their individual selves. Those who cannot reach outside of themselves face a sense of isolation and stagnation, the eventual experience of many takers. In Christian traditions, too, making a contribution is usually considered essential to inner peace and to a sense of sharing in a greater love outside of oneself.

So takers miss out on more than just their fair share of the available goodies. Those who focus narrowly on themselves also miss out on the inner contentment that comes from nurturing and being nurtured in a loving relationship.

Takers who can see the futility of living only for themselves may wish to consider some suggestions for change. Those who see that their selfishness harms those close to them face a tremendous challenge and must be willing to persist through some uncomfortable revelations. They are in for some tough times and should be as gentle with themselves as possible.

Where should they begin? Those who fear they are being cheated might do well to tally their blessings. Takers are so concerned with what is being withheld from them that they miss out on what is theirs already, freely given. Look closely at what your husband or wife contributes to make your life better. Look for signs of generosity and good faith. Perhaps it is not everything you want, but allow it to count for something. Take some time each day to note the little things your beloved does for you, and to appreciate them. Perhaps you can find in your heart a feeling of gratitude for what is given. Don't duck it! Dwell on it. Allow yourself to experience it, along with whatever awkwardness or sadness comes with it. You may remember earlier times in your relationship when you really appreciated how your beloved helped you and supported you. Some of that same experience may be there to be recaptured, but that will happen by gentle appreciation, not angry accusation.

Appreciating what is given already makes you more than merely a taker. Genuine appreciation is itself a gift that can support and nourish the one who is trying to please you. Showing appreciation can help rebalance a relationship.

You cannot express appreciation for what you are given and at the same time complain convincingly that you receive too little and must have more. Experiencing the one thus means letting go of the other. Figure out for yourself if the trade-off is worth it for you.

Takers who do not want to change their basic outlook might do better with a simpler suggestion. You are more likely to get whatever you want from your partner with civility than with complaints. So pace yourself and plan for the long haul. Don't throttle the goose that lays the golden egg.

Love Is to Be Shared. Support and nurturance must go both ways in a relationship if love is to remain fresh and vital. Those who are basically generous but are not nurtured in return gradually wear down, losing the joy that once made their giving so special. In turn, those who are nurtured but then contribute nothing become increasingly narcissistic, taking it all for granted. Love that is given must also be received, to complete the simplest transaction. And once received it must then be returned so that supplies remain replenished and may be given again. The best arrangements thus form a loop, in which each partner gives and receives freely so that the flow between them remains strong.

As in an electric circuit, any one break in the connection can prevent the flow of energy. Love that is given both ways returns to each to be shared further and so builds upon itself. While it is easy to see just givers and just takers as good guys and bad guys, each of these characters is limited in an important way that creates particular problems for their partners. Husbands and wives must each be willing both to give and to take if something special is to grow from the nurturance between them.

PART

III

Anger Makes Its Mark

> When angry, count to ten before you speak; if very angry, a hundred.
>
> —Thomas Jefferson

> When angry, count four; when very angry, swear.
>
> —Mark Twain[1]

Anger reigns freely in many a marriage, weakening the spirit of cooperation and hardening the hearts of the supposed intimates. Too many angry hours or angry years together do not subdue anger but tighten its grip and make it more stubborn.

However uncomfortable we are with anger and however much we may want to ignore it or swallow it, some anger persists in spite of our wishes. What are we to do with our anger? An apparent truism of modern popular psychology is that to get over angry feelings, we must vent them—express and thereby release them at the appropriate target. Otherwise, it is said, the anger will stay bottled up like steam in a sealed cooker, causing inner turmoil and imbalances and affecting the quality of our mental health for the worse.

There may be something to this. We all know of long-suffering people who fail to express their anger and so hold it inside and seethe. Unwilling to admit they are angry, they are nonetheless consumed by anger, most obviously to those around them. Yet we also know of angry people who are quite the opposite—who condemn and lash out at those around them again and again and who remain just as angry or become even angrier through volatile outbursts. There seems to be something true and important about expressing our angry feelings, but there may also be something false and troublesome about it as well.

Traditional Christianity lists anger as a deadly sin, advocating caution and tight control over it, while our modern pundits of mental health preach that anger is normal and must be expressed. No wonder so many are so confused about what to do, both with their own anger and with the anger of those around them. Should we combine the good advice of Thomas Jefferson and Mark Twain? Should we count to a hundred, then swear?

Despite its ambiguities and complexities, anger has an inner logic of its own. A few simple concepts do much to clarify the nature of anger and to untangle the contradictions and misunderstandings.

Anger is expressed in many forms. It can be as obvious as a slap in the face, or as subtle and sneaky as a catty remark artfully camouflaged almost to pass as a compliment. While some anger is provoked by grievous wrongs and intolerable injustices, other expressions of it appear unjustified, irrational, narrow minded, or petty. Anger may be freely and openly expressed, or it may be held inside as one tries to control it. Angry outbursts can be impulsive, like uncontrolled temper tantrums, or they can be quite calculated, as when a spoiled brat—even a grown-up spoiled brat—loses his temper for effect, knowing just when to lose it and how long to keep it lost, then is smugly satisfied when he gets his way. Anger can be beneficial, propelling us to assert ourselves and uphold our rights. But it is just as often harmful, both to those it lashes out at and to the individual who is angry.

The next chapters discuss the many variations of anger, showing how anger makes sense and the roles it plays in our lives. The patterns analysis reveals how anger perpetuates itself in intimate relationships, then suggests straightforward principles for managing anger and overcoming the patterns. The proper question is not whether you should express your anger but how to express it to your advantage. The case histories should make clear what is right and what is wrong about various expressions of anger, and which are beneficial and which are harmful. Seek to acquire some practical ways to channel your anger, to gain advantages from it, and to avoid the unnecessary animosities that so often echo in its wake.

6

Is Your Anger Justified?

During my clinical training at the University of Colorado at Boulder, I was again and again faced with angry clients and with problems of trying to understand them. Amid classroom banter about psychologically sophisticated interpretations of anger, which attributed it to everything from unconscious impulses to family constellations, one instructor had the audacity to ask the simplest and most obvious question: "What is this person mad about?" It seemed too easy to ask about the specific circumstances: "What is the grievance?" "What provokes his anger?" "What is going wrong for her that makes her angry?" Yet this question opened a door that led us further into the heart of the matter than any of the more complicated theories about anger. Surely an angry person is angry about something; nobody is angry about nothing at all.

One obvious way to try to calm an inappropriately angry person is to challenge his very justification for being angry. We might try to clarify the situation for him, to show that things are not really as unfair as he feels they are. When he no longer feels so mistreated, his anger may subside. Such challenges to anger can sometimes be successful—but only sometimes. Only anger that is based on a simple misperception will subside when the misperception is corrected. But when something more is involved, which is more often than not, the challenge fails. Those who are frequently angry tend to feel truly mistreated and will not be talked out of it easily. If we persist in trying, the already-angry person feels we are siding against him and gets angry at us as well.

So in talking with angry husbands and wives, I usually concede at the beginning that they have some justification for their anger. I first try to understand their concerns and to legitimize their grievances for them. Then we figure out where to go from there.

Anger Is Always Justified

Marriages have a paradoxical quality of bringing forth both the best and the worst in human nature. With our beloved we share our strongest passions and our deepest loyalties, but we share our darkest and most uncivil sides as well. Our most intense anger is more apt to be directed at one whom we apparently love the most than toward a mere friend or acquaintance. A marriage or other intimate involvement demands more of us than a simple friendship does. Trust is more important in more intimate relationships, and there are therefore more possibilities for that trust to be violated. A friend can disappoint you, but only someone you love can break your heart.

Any normal real-life marriage provides about as many justifications for anger as you or I or anyone else might wish. You entrust your beloved with your needs for support and understanding, your worst fears and your noblest ideals, your sexual identity, your longings and ambitions, your very future. Since your partner, like everyone, is imperfect and fallible, the possibilities that you will be hurt somewhere are almost limitless. So whatever the condition of your marriage, you no doubt have some justification for anger.

But anger is not always *well* justified. People overreact to minor troubles, and some of the reasons people get angry might be considered small, petty, trivial, unreasonable, or unimportant by those around them. People sometimes reexamine their own reasons for their surge of anger after it passes, and find them trivial or unreasonable in retrospect. But once you conclude that your justifications are not so important, you usually calm down. I do not claim that people always have *good* reasons for getting angry, only that they always have *some* reasons. It is in this sense that one can say that anger is always justified. Anger is instigated by a grievance, an apparent provocation, an overt insult, a subtle inconsiderateness, a minor wrong, or a major injustice. Anger is triggered by something perceived at the time to be worth getting angry over. In the heat of the emotion—to yourself, at least—your anger is always justified (figure 6–1).

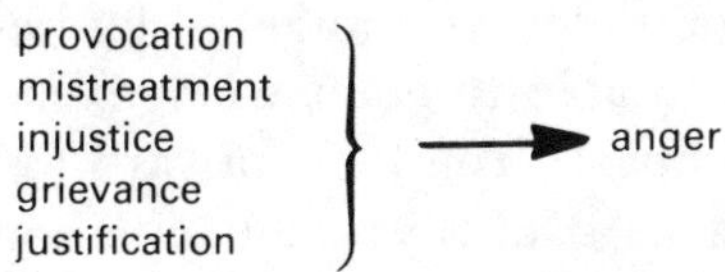

Figure 6–1. Grievances Provoke Anger

The connection between grievances and anger has been noted by cultures over many generations. The ancient Roman philosopher-statesman Seneca identified anger as a process sparked by a perceived injury or hurt or by an affront;[1] the Stoics saw anger as aimed at one whom you deem to have injured you unjustly. A modern survey found that both men and women are likely to feel that their anger is justified.[2] People feel themselves entitled to be angry because someone who wronged them "knew what he was doing" or "could have been more considerate and thoughtful" and thereby avoided causing the trouble. Most of us are apparently quite aware of what it is that makes us angry, at least much of the time.

Anger can also be caused by a string of minor reversals, any of which taken by itself is not particularly significant but that add up to something that is significant when taken together. The last reversal may stand out as the proverbial straw that overloaded the beast and provoked the breakdown. It is not only socks left on the floor that causes the anger, but the strewn socks piled on top of a long backlog of too much work and too little appreciation. Perhaps no one incident in particular seems noteworthy, and you find yourself angry, but you do not know why. Your inability to identify your grievance does not mean that everything is fair and right and that therefore you have no grievance. An angry person always has a grievance.

Perceived grievances are linked so closely to anger that they can serve as signposts to identify anger. The chances are good that someone who parades a long list of grievances is angry, whether she admits it or not. Persons who cannot acknowledge their own anger can nonetheless be quite vocal about their grievances. One of the best ways to get people to accept their own anger, as psychotherapist Peter Ossorio suggests, is to legitimize their grievances.[3] That means to clarify for themselves what their grievances are.

A woman I counseled was angered by her husband working late, but she was unable to acknowledge that she was angry. I legitimized her feelings: "You look forward to being close to him, then it seems that he is always gone with something else to do. That's the sort of thing that might make anyone angry." Once she accepted that her grievance might make anyone angry, it was an easy step for her to admit that yes, it had made her angry as well. So by accepting her grievance as justified, she came to accept her anger as well.

People vary in what and how much is sufficient to get them angry. Easygoing types may readily overlook what appear to be serious provocations, while fast triggers are readily provoked by everyone and everything and by life itself. Generally, the seriousness of the grievance is a good gauge of the amount of anger. The more intolerable one perceives the alleged wrong to be, the more intense will be the anger.

The grievances that provoke anger are varied indeed. They include sins of omission and sins of commission, and they range from the obvious and commonplace to the subtle and obscure. One of the more typical grievances that married women have is that the husband is unattentive, inconsiderate, uncommunicative, and unemotional, and therefore (conclusion obvious), he does not really love her. It is a failure to do something that provides the grievance and the way it is interpreted. The husbands in these marriages may be angry at being trapped by too many unspecified expectations.

Defensiveness. Even when anger is defensive, it still feels as if it has been provoked. The principle behind defensive anger is simple: defensive persons figure that the best defense is a good offense, so they lash out at those who might otherwise lash out at them first. People who are defensive feel that they are vulnerable to being accused and blamed. They anticipate accusations and may readily interpret innocent comments as implying that they did something wrong. If they feel vaguely guilty, they also feel persecuted and wronged by any suggestion that they are guilty or that it is their fault. Any accusation is arbitrary and unfair, they feel, so they have a right to defend themselves against it.

A wife who takes offense at the slightest suggestion that she has done something wrong thereby prevents anyone from criticizing whatever she does. She may have often been berated as a youngster and learned that criticism is ill founded and capricious and that she has a right to fight back. She prefers to push her inconsiderate husband off balance, lest he find fault with her when she is least expecting it.

An alcoholic husband who finds grave fault with his wife for any and every inconvenience thereby counters her accusation that it is he and demon rum who are ruining their marriage. He blames her for the murkiness inside that impels him to drink and therefore feels justified in knocking the legs out from under her as she swings at him.

One who is under attack clearly has a right to defend himself. The same seems to be true for those who merely anticipate an upcoming attack or misperceive something as an attack that was not meant that way. Justifications for our anger come from reality as we perceive it.

Rights. Having a grievance implies that there is some standard of how we ought to be treated that was not met. The wife who is angry because her husband is not more involved with her believes that she has a right to expect him to be more involved. The husband who resents his wife because she is too plain considers that he has a right to have a more glamorous partner. More generally, whenever we are angry, we believe—at least implicitly—that we have a right to a better bargain. At that moment we believe that we are the sort of folks who should not have to be troubled with the failings and inconsiderateness that others hand our way.

To understand how anger is justified, we should look more closely at the rights we feel we do or should have in a marriage that are not being respected. Some rights are critically important, and some we may be willing to relinquish for the sake of getting along.

Bookkeeping. Many grievances are painfully obvious, but some hide themselves and play peek-a-boo, aggravating us without being identified and labeled in our conscious minds. At this point in your investigation, take a moment to make sure you can clearly identify

- your own grievances that are the causes of your anger
- the rights you feel you have to be treated better

You may find it useful to write out a list of your grievances and your corresponding rights that are not being respected.

To gain some balance and to broaden your perspective, you might also look at the grievances your husband or wife has against you, and at the rights that he or she feels you are violating. List these as well, and compare them with the list of your own grievances.

Whose list is longer? Which grievances seem to you to be more substantial and more justified?

Yours? Are you surprised?

Anger Justifies Itself

Anger expresses itself in accusations that make the initial grievances seem as convincing as possible. Anger thus perpetuates itself by strengthening its own sense of justification.

When you are angry, the everyday inconsiderateness you encounter seems more obvious and intrusive than usual. You are less patient, less tolerant, and more apt to get rattled by minor annoyances that you would otherwise overlook. Anger attunes you to see provocations and to respond to them with more anger. When you are furious, your cat rubbing against your leg can be annoyingly intrusive. Your husband or wife hardly stands a chance. Literally anything someone does might be the wrong thing at any time. Although grievances lead to anger, anger in turn sensitizes us to additional grievances, fanning the flames.

When angry, most of us work to build a case against whomever we feel has done us wrong. Who is right and who is wrong is not always obvious, even in calmer moments when we are all trying to be fair about it. In the heat of anger, it is open season. Right and wrong become matters of opinion as adversaries blindly argue their own cases and counter challenges from their opponents.

It is to our advantage to put the blame elsewhere, as there is an obvious gain in being right and an obvious loss in being wrong. When you perceive yourself at fault, you feel guilty or at least humbled by your mistakes, while you can feel justified and righteous when someone else is at fault. So most of us are willing to do our share to make sure the blame passes us and lands on someone else who is a handy target.

When you feel you have been treated unfairly, you want the wrongdoer to acknowledge the troubles he or she has caused you and to treat you better in the future. Most of us are willing to go to some lengths to get that to happen.

In the illustration that follows, a woman is accusing her husband. The same justification principles obviously apply to men and women equally.

Married now just over a year, Jill has been feeling that her husband Jeremy is taking her completely for granted. Were she calm and feeling good about him, she might mention to him that he has not seemed as interested in doing things together as he used to be and ask him if anything is wrong. She might mention that while he does spend some time with her, which she appreciates, she would like more. And she would make some suggestions about what she would like to do with him or ask him what he might like to do together. Her perspective would be relatively balanced, first crediting her husband with what he does for her already and then asking for more. She would not be making an accusation that it is entirely his fault or that he is treating her badly and so owes her. In asking this way, she would have to rely on his willingness to listen and to choose on his own to be more involved.

That is how we might argue it were we calm and collected and in a conciliatory mood. But that is not how most of us argue when we are upset—especially not when we are very angry. When we are furious, we argue that we have been sorely mistreated and that it is intolerable and inexcusable. We want to make the strongest case possible against our antagonist, saying that he or she is being unfair and rightfully owes us much more than has been forthcoming. Any attempt to balance the presentation and give even coverage to both sides of the story might seem to weaken our argument, and we want the strongest argument possible.

Making unbalanced arguments requires making only a few easy choices in selection and emphasis. When angry, we focus narrowly on what someone has done to us and ignore whatever we may have done in return. An angry memory is always a selective memory. Jill has been ignored too long, and by now she is very angry. She selectively attends to the hardships Jeremy has handed her and builds them into a case against him, overlooking the hardships that she causes for him. Angry that her husband is late again and has forgotten to phone, she does not take into consideration the grief she usually gives him when he does finally get home or the thoughtful gift he gave her for her birthday. At other times she might, but not now when she is furious at him.

Ordinary grievances are readily expanded in the heat of anger in order to strengthen the force of the accusation. The words *always* and *never* are well-suited to the task. "You never want to just talk to me!" Jill snaps. "You never want to be around me! You always think of yourself first!" And so it goes. "You always leave the toilet seat up!" The hotter the anger, the more apt we are to broaden and exaggerate the grievances.

Intangibles can be included, and can add protection because they are almost impossible to refute. "You don't care anything about my feelings," Jill complains. "You don't love me anymore." The subject of the argument goes from tangible actions, such as interrupting or not paying attention, to a broad condemnation based on inner attitudes and feelings. The justifications increase quickly. Jill considers that if her husband cared for her or loved her at all, he would not continue to do as he does but would change and do what she wants. She takes his refusal to change as proof positive that he does not love her anymore.

Most accusations are not so calculated, but seem to blurt freely from the heat of the moment. Yet neither are they entirely unrehearsed. Most of us mull over our grievances and usually contemplate a confrontation, thereby preparing ourselves for a possible showdown. We anticipate what we would say, what someone might say back, and how we would answer in return. Mulling over our grievances is thus a rehearsal for an upcoming argument.

People who are nervous about the upcoming confrontation may go over their justifications many times, wanting to be fully prepared.

We Believe Our Own Propaganda. Making accusations—the actual confrontations and our mental rehearsals for them—are intensely involving experiences. Our anger increases until it is ready for release. Fear lingers in the shadows, adrenaline pumps through our bloodstream, our focus narrows. The consequences are uncertain, and our future is on the line. Those so involved in making angry accusations must rely on the strength of their justifications for what seems to be their very survival. Not surprisingly, angry people come to believe more strongly in their own justifications. When justifications are fair and reasonable, it is good to believe in them. When justifications are one-sided and unbalanced, as many are, angry people are carried off course by their own arguments. Their justifications are a form of propaganda, as much as anything, that has been generated to stake a claim and win an argument. After people mentally rehearse their propaganda to use against their opponents, they get taken in themselves and become convinced of their own propaganda.

A press secretary, it is said, tells tales of convenience to gullible reporters, sleeps soundly, then comes to believe his own tales when he reads them the next day in the papers. An angry person, too, culls his or her own easy justifications, uses them to strengthen an accusation, then comes to truly believe in them.

Studies in social psychology confirm this principle, finding that as people prepare positions and argue them aloud, they thereby convince themselves of their merits.[4] The freer they are to choose their positions, the more they believe in their arguments.

When Jill yells tearfully at her husband that he does not love her anymore, she is not merely expressing her feelings. She is scripting and then participating in an intensely involving experience. As she makes her wild accusations, she feels anger and sadness over her terrible misfortune. Perhaps she fears the life alone that could surely follow. So while her accusation is aimed at her husband, it hits herself as well, leaving her at least as injured by it as her husband. And the more she repeats it and the more convincingly, the more she too is wounded by the message it contains. The more she believes that he cares nothing for her, the more justifications she has for anger.

The pattern is selective justifications, followed by accusations, belief in the justifications, further anger, and more justifications. The pattern perpetuates itself (figure 6–2).

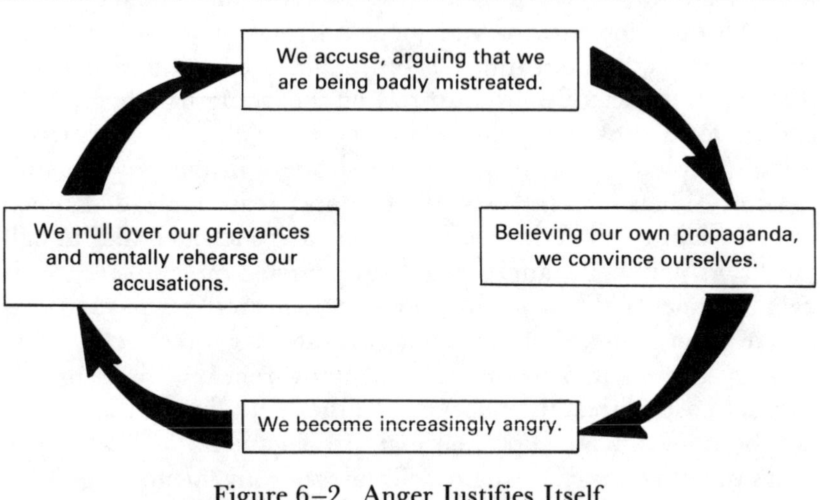

Figure 6–2. Anger Justifies Itself

Our Own Justifications Are More Immediate. Accusations invite counteraccusations, and in a fair quarrel your own justifications are answered by the case your spouse presents against you. But opposing accusations usually do little to soften anger, especially when the anger is intense and the arguments heated. In the midst of a screamer, husband and wife are so focused on making their own justifications that they understand little or nothing of what the other is saying. While she is accusing him, he is so involved in preparing his counterarguments that he never seriously considers her grievances. He waits for his turn to talk, or he interrupts. Then, while he is accusing her, she puts her attention on preparing her counteraccusations and misses his concerns. In the heat of an argument, they hear only their own arguments, and thus become further convinced of their own justifications.

Anger on both sides creates justifications that are even more one-sided. Look at your own beliefs on how much damage is caused by your anger. Normally, we have one view of our own anger and another view of our mate's anger. It all depends on whether we are dishing it out or taking it in the chest. We all know how much anger hurts when someone lashes out at us—we experience that directly. And when an intimate lashes out at us, it hurts even more. But most of us tend to overlook how much our own anger hurts others. In an argument, one typically conceals vulnerabilities and weaknesses, making it hard for us to see just how deeply our words have cut. And any indications of hurt are usually well cloaked in anger, inviting us to fight on. So when husbands and wives quarrel, they experience only their own injuries and are blind to the way their anger hurts the other. And their perception is therefore that they alone are being injured in the argument and that their insensitive adversary is getting off free. This apparent injustice provides them both with further grounds for anger.

When and if we do recognize the harm our anger causes, this can be justified as well. Rather than feel guilty or penitent, which would be humbling, we can blame the consequences of the fight on the adversary, who obviously caused it. The more harm we have done, the more we have to justify. Those who have hurt each other over the course of many years would be overwhelmed by this responsibility, and they avoid facing it. Instead, they cling to their justifications as if therein lies their salvation.

Quick Anger and Lingering Anger. Justifications are often suited to the form of anger one typically expresses. Suppose the wife expresses anger quickly and openly, while the husband is slower but more persistent with it. She yells her heart out, then she is over it and wants him over it as well. He shows little anger while she yells at him but then holds it against her for days afterward. She feels that her yelling is justified since she is only expressing her feelings, which she believes is healthy to do; afterward, she is willing to forgive and forget and be pleasant. He is the one who is causing the problem now, she feels, because he sits on his feelings and holds a grudge for so long. But he feels that he is the one who is justified, not her. After all, she is the one who flies at him over almost nothing, blasts him up one side and down the other before he knows what is happening, then expects him to forget about it and be pleasant. Although she has beaten him in the initial battle, he does not have to let her get away with it.

The roles may be reversed, of course: The husband may be quicker and better with open anger, and the wife may be the one left to seethe about how he rolled over her. Regardless of gender, the one who gets the best in the initial outburst feels it ought to be over with afterward, while the one who loses holds the grudge.

Justifications to Friends. In an important variation, the accusations are bandied about with friends and acquaintances who are willing to listen. A wife who complains to her women friends that her husband is inattentive or unfaithful may be assured of their sympathy and support if they have similar grievances against their own partners. In such circumstances, she is unlikely to be challenged by anyone standing up for her husband or pointing out that she herself would be hard to live with. Together, the friends and the wife collaborate to build a consensus that the men in question are not merely fallible but worthless and insensitive. Everyone agrees in supporting one side of what might otherwise be mistaken for a two-sided relationship. Supporting each other's grievances, they further convince themselves of their own justifications. The wife then carries the bitterness so generated back into the routine of her marriage.

Improve Your Justifications

To moderate our anger, we might try to gain a better perspective on the grievances that produce it and the justifications for it. The following suggestions may help clarify some common but troublesome justifications for anger.

What Is the Point? Persistent accusations gain credibility from the continual repetition of their self-serving message. Recognizing your motives for your accusations can be important in calming your self-perpetuating justifications.

When I see married couples tangled in accusations and counteraccusations, I usually begin by pointing out to them the limited ambitions of their interactions: "You are each working to show that it is the other one who is at fault here. Jill, you are saying that Jeremy is rude to you in front of friends, to show that it is he who is causing the problems and that you are justified therefore in being angry at him. And Jeremy, you are saying that Jill is cold to and angry at you, to show it is she who is hard to be around and that you are justified in being angry at her. Do you realize that you are both spending time arguing over who is at fault and who is justified? Do you realize that all you are saying is that it is the other who is to blame, not you?"

And then I go to practicalities: "Are you going to get anywhere this way?" Most people may need a few reminders to be able to recognize when something they say is merely an accusation. But most people can see that making these accusations is not getting them anywhere and is not likely to do so in the near future.

Questions of who is at fault are usually complicated far beyond our most tangled nightmares. If we really wanted to focus there, we could spend a long time doing so and would ultimately have nothing to show for it. We could reconstruct scene after scene and analyze the interactions closely, then make a tally sheet of credits for the good we have done and debits for the harm we have caused. And after we have spent many hours or days or weeks on this, what would we have? After all that labor, our conclusions are not likely to be clearer than when we started. And if our partner still refuses to see the wisdom of our conclusions, do we do it all over again? By this point, most people get the picture.

***Always* and *Never*.** Accusations that are overblown in the heat of anger can be moderated to achieve better outcomes. The words *never* and *always* almost always invite resistance and are usually not true. Typically, we use *always* and *never* because they seem to make an accusation stronger, more forceful, more final. One who *always* does something is obviously the culprit and has little leeway to squirm out of it by claiming that it was just once or twice, or inadvertent, or not very important. We exaggerate to strengthen our claims, to gain the upper hand right off, and to preempt a lengthy argument over whether the grievances are really as bad as we ourselves know they are.

An overstated case usually accomplishes just the opposite of what it is meant to accomplish. An obvious exaggeration makes an argument less credible, not stronger. Since *never* and *always* arguments are not completely true, it is easy for the opponent to dismiss them as simply false. The kernel of truth that the overblown case may contain is overlooked. An overblown accusation is offensiv to the one on the receiving end of it because it seems unfair, and the one so accused becomes angry. It invites resistance rather than cooperation, and counteraccusation rather than understanding.

You usually expect to benefit from making your accusations, or why would you trouble yourself to make them? This expectation is usually implicit, and it can be helpful to identify it: What do you expect to accomplish by your complaints? The one who you say is in the wrong is the one who should have to change, and the main purpose of most accusations is to show that person that he is in the wrong and so bring pressure upon him to change and do what you want. Your expectation is that your accusation can force the person to change by convincing him that your accusation is justified.

Identify your purpose, then look at the outcome of your argument. Do your accusations work for you as you expect them to? If not, why not?

Would it help if you were more clever, more forceful, or more persistent? You may have been as clever as the language allows, and forceful enough already. How long will you continue to use the same tactic before you judge it a failure and try something else?

Try to state your grievances carefully and fairly. This will not weaken your position but will, in fact, make it stronger and more credible. You are much more likely to be taken seriously when you say only what you mean to say, and no more. The hype is unnecessary—mere garbage, obscuring your important message with its noise and clutter. You will do better without it. You might also try to balance your own concerns with those of your mate and thereby further increase the likelihood that you will be heard and understood.

When you are careful with the truth, you clarify your own thinking. You rebalance the mental scales that you use to weigh your marriage. You come to see your grievances for what they are, important in their own way but not the catastrophes you were blowing them up to be.

Answering an Exaggeration. Now take the other side. When you must answer an accusation, even an overblown one, it is important that you hear those aspects of the accusation that are well founded. When your partner gripes that you are "always" late, try to overlook the *always* and focus instead on the legitimate concern. "Well, surely not always," you might begin. "But you are saying that I am frequently late, and that it bothers you. Let me think about that for a minute." Your response should make your partner feel understood, and focusing on the always need not sidetrack you from focusing on the real concerns between you.

People tend to repeat accusations until they feel their partner has heard them. If you can accept part of an accusation, you lower the pressure your partner feels to continue forcing it upon you to get you to listen. Acknowledging that you hear your partner's side moves the battle a step forward, from focus on accusation to negotiation (and perhaps resolution).

Just the Facts (about Feelings). When your partner does something that rubs you the wrong way, it may be worth it to ask who should be held responsible for your ruffled feelings. Some say that you are really responsible, since your feelings are your own and you are the only one who is ever responsible for your feelings. I would not want to take it that far. Couples live too closely together for them to pretend that they do not strongly affect the way each other feels. But too often, we hold our mates fully responsible for bad feelings when we ourselves contribute our share to our own misery. At such times, attributing the responsibility to our mates is misplaced. By holding the other person responsible, we overlook our own contributions and do not put our own houses in order.

How can we check to see that we are assigning responsibility fairly? A problem stated as an accusation has already assigned the responsibility to the accused. The one who is angry might postpone making the accusation for a moment and present only the problem and the feelings that go with it.

A young wife was angry because her husband was an hour late getting home from work and accused him of not caring about her feelings. What is going on? It happened that this particular woman was terrified that her husband would be in an automobile accident and was worried sick by the time he finally walked in the door. When she saw that he was safe, she blamed him for her own feelings, saying that he should have been more considerate of her and come home when he said he would.

Was she justified in holding him responsible? Perhaps, but she would have done better to postpone doing so for a moment and tell her husband just what had happened. "When you came home later than you said you would," she might have told him, "I worried that you were in an accident. I began to wonder when you were ten minutes late, and by the time you were an hour late, I was really coming unglued over it." Once she had explained the problem, she could go on to ask that he be more careful to get home on time in the future. She might also recognize that her worries are extreme and that she might try to control her tendency to worry. The problem then becomes a shared responsibility, and both she and her husband can do something about it.

Such statements of feelings have been called "I" messages by Thomas Gordon, in his writings on parent and teacher effectiveness training.[5] I would prefer to call them "I feel" messages, since they state how "I feel" and what is going on that contributes to how "I feel." Harriet Lerner has prescribed such statements to break the "dance of anger."[6] In using them, you focus attention on yourself and not on whomever would otherwise be the target of your anger. You use them to talk about your feelings and to ask that you be understood and taken seriously. "I feel" messages express feelings respectfully in an atmosphere relatively free from the accusations that usually accompany anger.

Concerns expressed without accusation are more likely to be heard and understood. At the same time, it *is* important that you state your grievances and not just sit on them. Stating grievances helps you clarify them in your own mind, and talking them out helps put them in perspective. Realize that grievances may be quite legitimate and that you have the right to air them and have them taken seriously. It may be possible to identify what makes you mad and to try to negotiate a solution in an atmosphere of respect and cooperation. There are no guarantees, but it is possible sometimes, and it is surely worth a try.

Helpful Friends. Friends who lend an ear to be helpful should be careful about how much they add to the sense of justification. As a friend you want to be supportive, but it is easy to be taken in by one side of the argument and lose your sense of balance and fair play for the other party. You do no one a favor by assisting a complaining friend in messing up a manageable marriage. The trick is to listen and accept, but to remain as impartial as possible on the accusations. Reflective statements are helpful. Try, "You feel he does not listen when you talk to him," or, "You are troubled by how he acts when you are with friends." Avoid saying "Why, that jerk! You ought to leave him!" If you find yourself in over your head, be courageous enough to bail out. Suggest a pastor or a marriage counselor.

Accusations often have a variety of additional aims, as do other angry actions as well. Our investigation looks next at purpose and how it channels our expressions of anger.

7

A Method to the Madness

Like all human actions, those that arise from anger have some aim or purpose. Granted, purpose is more easily overlooked in these actions than in actions that arise from a calmer frame of mind. Anger is an impulse, and we can act out of anger impulsively with no planning and no sense of trying to gain anything by it. Some angry actions seem irrational or foolish, causing more trouble than they are worth, and some individuals find their anger unmanageable and frightening.

Actions that arise from other emotions also have functions. Guilt, for instance, functions to pressure us to avoid doing what we perceive as wrong, or to suffer or make amends for it. And fear, of course, motivates us to avoid or escape from an apparent danger. Consider a soldier who is overtaken by fear in the heat of battle, and runs. His act of running may be completely unplanned—perhaps he had wanted to prove his courage and his loyalty to his comrades and to his country. But although his act is impelled by unmanageable fear, it is not without purpose. Clearly, one runs from battle in order to escape the danger. The soldier may take a bullet in the back while running, but that is simply another case in which an act does not achieve its intended outcome. The purpose of the act was still to avoid the hazard of battle.

Human actions are not haphazard but are taken in order to accomplish something that one wants to accomplish. What is an angry action trying to accomplish?

Is the purpose of an angry outburst to "express your anger," as is so often said? Yes, surely an open expression of anger is meant to express the anger. But that is only a restatement of the obvious.

One might say too that the purpose of a frightened act is to express the fear, but clearly it is meant to do more than that. Its purpose is to avoid something frightening. And surely something as complicated as anger is meant to do more than merely express itself.

Emotional actions are usually meant to contend with the situation that causes the emotion. Just as an act of fear is meant to avoid that which is frightening, angry acts are meant to deal with that which provokes the anger. How does an angry act contend with the apparent mistreatment?

Anger Confronts

Ordinarily, angry actions serve to confront whoever caused the anger. An angry statement is usually an accusation, specifying who did what wrong and that the wrong is unacceptable. Some angry actions fail to specify what is wrong, assuming it is known or leaving one to guess. The force of angry action is usually uncomfortable for those on the receiving end, who experience it as pressure to change their behavior.

Anger itself propels us to confront. Anger motivates us to stand up for ourselves, to challenge wrongs, and to assert our rights. Anger adds power to our voice, saying that we mean business for sure and cannot be put off or ignored.

The physiological arousal that accompanies fear and anger prepares us for "fight or flight." Fear prepares us for flight, and anger prepares us for a social or physical confrontation, which we may either act upon or control.

Perhaps surprisingly, the outcomes of angry confrontations can be beneficial. While few people find anger pleasant, grievances aired may be resolved. A study by researcher James Averill provides some interesting information.[1] Angry statements seem to be moderately successful in getting someone to recognize his or her fault, and can cause someone to gain more respect for the person who is angry. Forty percent of individuals faced with an angry confrontation claimed that they changed their actions because of it. Accused of being late, perhaps four in ten men would try to come home on time. Women accused of ignoring a husband when with friends would try to be more attentive next time in about the same percentage.

But many people who face angry accusations do not so readily accept that it is their fault, or at least not *all* their fault. About half those confronted with anger bolstered their own justifications in opposition to the accusation. And overall, it seems anger may be quite harmful to a relationship. Three in ten said that they lost respect for the person who got angry at them, or that their relationship grew more distant because of an angry episode. And the majority, a sturdy six in ten of those confronted with an angry accusation, did *not* change to accommodate an angry partner. Unfortunately, the typical outcome of an angry outburst is that people continue in doing whatever it was that originally provoked the anger, but in addition they resent the one who got angry at them.

Anger Punishes. In one ongoing tangle, the husband overworks and the wife is angered by his lack of involvement with her. Over the course of many years, Angela and Chuck have related as pursuer and distancer. Irritated by his typical absence, Angela readily berates him for being gone or is cold and moody when she is with him. And Chuck takes refuge whenever possible in anything that takes him away from her.

Angela finally convinces him to go with her to a Valentine's dinner and dance, and so she has him all to herself for a whole evening with no interruptions. In the beginning, Chuck makes the best of his fate and acts the proper gentleman. It could be a good time for both of them, were they able to forget their past arguments and live in the moment. But grievances seem to have lives of their own.

The romantic atmosphere is just what Angela has wanted, but it reminds her of all she has been missing over the years. The dinner is excellent, and the two of them dance several slow numbers together, close and warm, just like old times. She goes for a restroom break, and she returns to find that Chuck has gone off somewhere. She cannot locate him. She feels hurt and abandoned—and angry. Wandering after him is just one more reminder of her life of waiting for him. She finally finds him chatting on the sidelines with one of his business associates. She moves into the circle of the conversation and finds that he is deep into a lengthy discussion about a golf weekend. "Sorry, fellows, he's mine for the evening," she chirps cheerfully, taking him by the hand and leading him away from the conversation.

So far, so good—apparently. Chuck does not seem to mind being recaptured, actually admiring her pluck and social grace. Were Angela to leave it at that, the specialness of the night might continue. But by now, she is much too angry at him and she wants to express it. She leads him out onto the back patio, where she has him alone for a moment. "How was I supposed to know where you were?" she scolds. "You act like you have no idea I even exist!"

That does it! Involved in his conversation, Chuck had not really considered that she might be looking for him. So her anger seems to be coming from nowhere, and he does not appreciate it. He might have let her know where he was, but that is no justification for the anger that she now slams at him. He sees her as moody, grouchy, hard to be around—just the same here as at home. If he could apologize and reach out to her now, the specialness of the night could continue. But he feels wronged and is not about to apologize. Trapped for the moment with no exit, he sulks. While Angela wants them to appear the loving couple in front of their friends, Chuck belittles her and jokes snidely that she cannot allow him out of her sight, which makes her all the angrier.

At two critical points here, anger propelled actions that wound up spoiling what might otherwise have been a warm and pleasant evening. After stealing him away from his business friends, Angela might have congratulated herself and enjoyed Chuck for as long as her limited lease on him permitted. But her anger was too strong, and it spoke for her. Staying pleasant would have meant letting him get away with one more instance of neglect, she felt, and her strong anger fought against that. She did not want him to think that that was all it took to placate her. He must not think that a single good evening could compensate for years of indifference, and she does not have to be a fortune-teller to know that all will continue tomorrow as usual. Anger wants to punish, and by scolding him she showed him there were consequences.

Chuck too had a choice. Confronted by his wife, he could have simply acknowledged that he had inconvenienced her and apologized for it. But he was hurt by her scolding more than he would admit, and he did not want to let her get away with it. Had he apologized and tried to placate her, he felt, he would just have been reinforcing her bad conduct.

And so the feud continues. Because he sulks and makes snide remarks, Angela is more convinced that he wants to avoid her, and because she is after him, Chuck is sure she is absolutely impossible. Her anger was plenty punishing, but nobody learned the right lesson from the punishment.

An angry action is not an impassioned appeal to good faith and fair play, but a tactic of confrontation. Any angry act that is meant to assert does so in a particularly contentious way—by hostility and attack—thereby laying the groundwork for lingering animosities.

Hostility is a retaliation for the wrongs that provoked the anger. When we are angered, we do not want to allow the person to go on his or her merry way and get away with it. If we did, nothing would keep that person from doing it again. We want to show that we are not a milquetoast or a wimp or a nobody who can be run over for free. The steam of anger propels us to retaliate for an injustice, rather than forgive and forget and let someone get away scot-free as though nothing had happened.

Assertive Actions and Hostile Actions. There is an important contrast between actions that are merely assertive and those that are hostile. Assertive acts are meant to benefit us by upholding our rights, while hostile acts strike out to punish someone who has wronged us. Punishment itself is socially sanctioned under the right circumstances, and it has two purposes: it aims to correct misconduct, and to extract a fair penalty for it. While simple assertion tries to uphold our rights, it seeks to avoid ruffling feathers any more than is necessary along the way. But punishment is meant to hurt, to inflict a just penalty for the misconduct and to provide a warning not to do it again.

The stronger our anger, unfortunately, the less we look out for ourselves and the stronger our inclination to punish. Carried along by bitterness or rage, it is easy to completely forget about gaining any benefit for ourselves at all. In its narrow focus on punishment, intense anger can propel us to wreck what we might otherwise cherish and seek to preserve.

Acknowledging the Aim of Anger Is Uncomfortable. I am inviting you here to grapple with the contentious underside of angry actions. Angry acts usually hurt, and the hurt is not merely incidental, as though the act were meant to be cordial and pleasant, but inadvertently miscarried and ruffled some feathers. Hostile actions *aim* to punish. Were a hostile act to cause no trouble at all, we would wonder if it had somehow missed its mark.

Those who are uncomfortable with their own anger—that is, most of us—may well be uncomfortable with this interpretation of anger's function. I usually get a lively response when I talk to community groups about anger, but I see a noticeable downturn in the mood when I mention that anger acts to punish. Most of us—especially those who are often angry—want our own anger to be innocent of such morally troublesome implications. People who feel mistreated want to be free to get angry, not to be burdened by someone calling it a sin.

I am sympathetic with them. I considered omitting some of this section altogether, or watering it down. But what could I substitute in its stead to make angry patterns make sense? Should I re-echo the position that an angry act is merely an expression of angry feeling, thereby making it personally acceptable by omitting the important questions of aims and consequences. I choose not to. Those who want only pleasant bromides can find a wide selection of them elsewhere, and I believe that it is better to grapple with the uncomfortable side of human nature. Otherwise we cruise along blindly in a cloud of illusion, only to curse our circumstances every time we crash.

Do remember that anger *is* human nature, to be understood and accepted and managed like any other aspect of human nature. I get angry, surely, and when I was younger I used to get angry more often than many people, more often than I would want to publicly admit. I was angry at my wife as much as at anyone, perhaps because we have always looked to each other for so much. Perhaps my anger was justified, as everyone's anger is in some ways; I recall that I always felt justified at the time, as we all do. But I am both cursed and blessed with the insight to see the contentiousness of my own anger, its purpose, and its accomplishments. By now, I can see all too easily the harm it has done. I wish both to accept myself as I am, and to recognize that everything I am is not just as it should be.

As you look at the purposes of your own angry acts, realize that they are normal and natural, and be gentle with yourself. Anger functions in you just about as it does in anyone else, which is not so terrible that you must close your eyes to it. But do look.

If you are uncomfortable with the punishing side of anger, look to the source of that anger. If you did not feel justified, you would not be angry in the first place!

Wanting to Square the Score Indicates Anger. Just as justifications indicate anger, so does the sweetness of the payback. To those I talk to who are angry but not conscious of it, I clarify their legitimate objectives for them: "But after all he's done to you, you can't just let him get away with it scot-free, can you!"

Those who are truly angry cannot say that they would want their mates to get away with it. One who has truly forgiven or forgotten and is no longer angry is no longer so concerned with the injustice of the matter. But as long as anger simmers, we do not want the transgressor to go unpunished.

The appeal of minor-league vengeance helps us clarify our angry patterns, because it makes sense of why we continue in a hostile manner in spite of the usually poor outcomes.

Anger Begets Contrariness

Angry actions may lead to a wide variety of outcomes, most of which are just what we do not want. In the best of circumstances, our anger acts to correct the problem, as our mate concedes the justness of our cause and complies to our wishes. But most adversaries are not so cooperative, and other outcomes are much more typical.

Ordinarily, anger provokes some form of opposition from its target. Someone who faces hostile accusation usually perceives it as unfair and unwarranted, as well as harmful and wrong in and of itself. Hostility marks at least a momentary lapse in warmth and civility and so always counts as something of a breach of the goodwill between partners. Those who do not accept all the blame—that is, most people much of the time—are offended or hurt by offhand accusations. Hostility seems an attempt to win by force of intimidation what could not be won by cooperation and fair play.

When Angela scolded him, Chuck saw it as antagonistic, unjustified, and unfair. So out of principle and ordinary obstinacy, he was not about to comply. Those who are targets of hostility see themselves as the wronged parties and are justified therefore in opposing their angry partners. Anger, when it is seen as unfair, begets not cooperation but contrariness. Unfortunately, *the one who is the target of the anger never considers it to be as justified as the one who is angry does*. So anger quickly generates an atmosphere of ill will, which leads to obnoxious countermeasures.

Countermeasures can take an absolutely fascinating variety of forms: One might argue forcefully against the accusation ("You're completely wrong!") or yield in sarcastic acquiescence ("Whatever you say, dear"). One might slide the conversation over to grievances of one's own ("You never do anything but gripe at me!"). The individual who does not fight back openly can always withdraw or sulk, and get back at the angry person that way. One can refuse to comply with even the most reasonable of requests, in a principled protest against the scolding received. Or, one can comply at the moment, but then conveniently forget the next time the pledge comes due. A serious scolding can get a husband to clean the dishes one time, but this outcome seldom carries over to the next meal. He just forgets, right? An accusation that she is a prude might get a wife into bed one night, but her sexual interest vanishes thereafter. She is just not interested, okay?

Resistance operates in so many subtle ways that it is hard to keep up with them all. Most of what we want from a marriage requires a freely given spirit of cooperation, and that is not ordinarily produced by the punishing force of hostile anger.

Which countermeasures are favored by your intimate adversary? Often, they are based on what gets a rise out of you. Miffed over being scolded, most of us lean toward countermeasures that require the least of us and cause the most trouble for our antagonist. That often means that we continue to do whatever it is that our mate is upset about, or do it more.

A wife who condemns her husband for not wanting to be close to her will find him more and more of a stranger as the seasons pass. He says he has nothing to say to her or that his interests take him elsewhere. The husband who berates his wife for spending too much money will find that she keeps on spending (always on things they "really" need).

In a typical tangle, grievances trigger hostility that the targeted partner sees as unfair and counters by further contrariness, thereby generating further justifications for anger. What goes around comes around. Those who have sufficient cause for anger acquire more cause precisely because of their anger. The pattern perpetuates itself (figure 7–1).

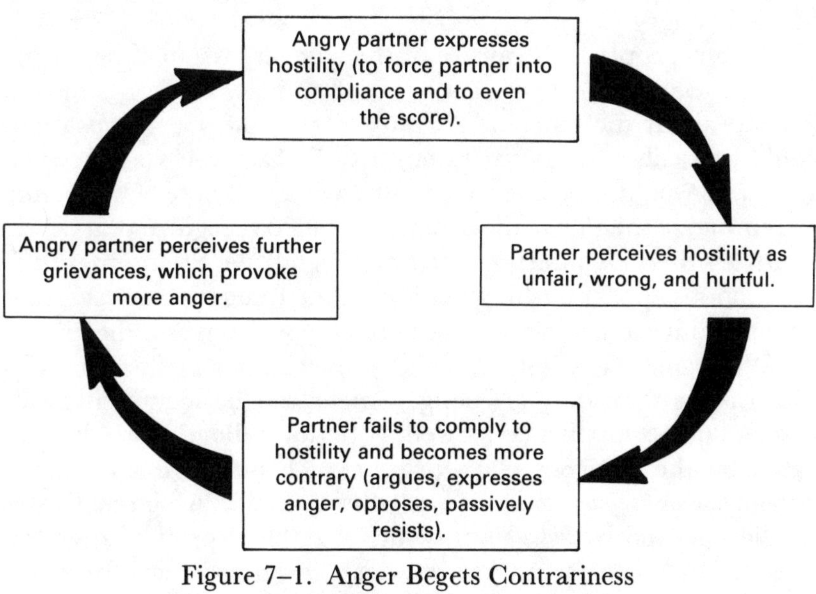

Figure 7–1. Anger Begets Contrariness

The more frequent the anger, the less the chance that it will ever produce compliance and cooperation. In an unusually angry atmosphere even the simplest and most reasonable request is likely to be ignored out of plain contrariness. Because it is spoken in anger, a request that would otherwise be accepted is adamantly refused. As impossible as it seems, angry mates seem to have absolutely no recognition at all that their own anger contributes to their problems, blaming everything on their awful spouses.

Our families and friends are quite sure that our anger is indeed part of the problem, just as are we sure that their anger toward us makes our own lives unpleasant. Most of us were condemned or punished for our anger while we were growing up, and we all must have learned that our own anger can spell trouble. So we may find it convenient to conceal or deny our anger, or at least to remain particularly inept at recognizing it.

Know Thyself. Most of us do recognize it when we are angry, but not all of us do. Some of us are inwardly angry and act in ways that others perceive as angry, but we do not recognize at all that we ourselves are angry. We may consider it wrong to be angry, are overwrought anyway, and do not want to be stigmatized by being labeled "angry."

To get people to be aware of their anger, I sometimes try to finesse the question of whether or not they really are angry and ask instead about the outcome: "Can you see how your accusations could be easily interpreted as hostility?" "Can you see that what you said would feel like an insult to her?" Those who cannot acknowledge their own anger may be able to recognize that others could legitimately interpret their acts as hostile. Seeing that their own actions appear hostile gives them something to go on and some responsibility to act in ways that do not come across as hostile.

While anger is a feeling, it should be obvious by now that it is much more than only a feeling.[2] Anger can be identified by its three major components, as well as by its feeling. Anger is indicated by the presence of *grievances,* which justify anger; by the person's *unwillingness to let someone get away with it,* which motivates retaliation; and by *hostile acts,* which are the imprint of anger on action. Anger is present when one has grievances, wants the transgressor punished, and acts in a hostile manner—regardless of whether one actually *feels* angry.

Try a slight variation on the question of being unaware of angry feelings. When you are angry, however you feel at that time *is* your feeling of anger. If you feel confused when you are angry, then for you, confusion is how it feels to be angry. Some people feel frightened when angry; others feel guilty. Many people feel upset when they are angry. And if you have no particular feelings at all when you are angry, then that is precisely what anger feels like for you.

Those who cannot readily identify their own feelings of anger are considered "out of touch" with their feelings, and the usual prescription is that they need to "get in touch" with their feelings. Some authorities propose that this be done by introspection, in which you look more closely for feelings that are hard to find; some suggest you learn to express your feelings more, to uncover them and get them out where you can see them. But identifying your own anger need not be so difficult. Those who do not feel feelings of anger per se can learn to identify one or more of its obvious components.

You might take a moment here to consider how to best recognize it when you are angry. Do you feel any telltale feelings at the time? Are they angry feelings or other feelings? Can you clearly identify your grievances at the moment? Can you flag your yearnings for justice, or your hostility? Figure out which of these are the best signals that you are angry. Look for them and learn to identify them quickly. Then you will be in reasonably good touch with your anger, whatever your feelings.

The next task is to learn to channel anger into more constructive outcomes.

Assertion Versus Retaliation

Our angry patterns are resolved best by acting on our healthy inclinations to look out for ourselves and not on our reflex impulses to punish. We calm our anger better by the intelligent assertion of our own best interests than by blind retaliation against an uncooperative mate. The two opposed factors are linked, like opposite sides of a playground see-saw. As we plan and implement assertion, our urge to retaliate subsides, but the trappings of retaliation must be suppressed for assertiveness to work properly. The one rises as the other falls. Those who invest their spirit in getting even seldom get ahead and are often left behind. In most marriages the path to getting ahead does not involve any amount of getting even. This suggests a new twist to the old saying, "Don't get even, get ahead."

Before you seek to rechannel your own anger, I suggest that you first take a look at your priorities. Remember something your husband or wife did that made you mad at the time and that can still make you mad. Remember how unfair it was, and experience once again the anger. Then consider the two sentences below. Mull the first one over in your mind for a minute, to see how it feels, then the second one.

- "After what he (she) has done, I cannot let him (her) get away with it."
- "After what he (she) has done, I want to find a way to prevent the problem from occurring again."

The first feeling motivates retaliation, and the second motivates assertion. Which strikes you more strongly? Does one appeal to your heart, while the other appeals to your head? Are you willing to forgo retaliation and settle on a plan of assertion and reconciliation?

Individuals like Angela and Chuck should look carefully at their choices and try to favor change over retaliation. Only then can they begin to step away from their patterns of anger and contrariness.

Make sure that your priorities are ordered as you wish them to be. Then consider your tactics.

Assess Your Tactics. While assertiveness must be tailored to fit a specific situation, the following general guidelines can be helpful. When you find yourself angry, give some thought to what you want out of the relationship. How do you want your partner to change? Your preferences here are ordinarily related to the grievances that provoke your anger. What you want is for your partner to stop doing whatever is making you mad. You want to be treated better, but be as specific as you can be. Angela wants her husband to be more attentive and to not belittle her in front of friends, or anywhere else. Chuck wants his wife to be calmer and more supportive and to not fly off at what seems like nothing at all.

Then project your wishes into a plan of action: How can you make what you want happen? While this seems like the obvious next step, for many people it is a stumbler. When we are angry, we all want someone else to change, not because we concede or coax but because that person has been unfair and owes it to us. Angela and Chuck both feel wronged and want the other to change. If you still believe someone will change just because he or she is unfair and you are mad about it, then realize that being mad about it *is* your plan of action. Perhaps it is not a very sophisticated plan, but it is your plan nonetheless. If it is not working and you follow it anyway, ask yourself what you are trying to get out of it. Do you really expect to get ahead with it, or are you just too stubborn to change? See if you are willing to let go, and try something new.

Several components can be woven together into a more hopeful plan of action. These suggestions include:

1. Present your grievances fairly
2. Play on your more human qualities
3. State what you want
4. Bargain for it

The statement of your grievances should be uninflated and fair, and balanced by your acknowledgment of your mate's side of the problem. Look now at the subtle force of the second suggestion.

Appear Human. It goes without saying that we are all genuine human beings. But I am concerned about appearing fully human, because in the heat of an argument we obviously have more important things on our minds, like winning. As much as anything else, anger goes a long way to make us forget about our common humanity. Faced with your hostility, your mate loses sight of your more sensitive qualities of love and tenderness. At that moment, he or she is more likely to see you as attacking, intimidating, unloving, self-centered, and perhaps mean or hateful—and treat you accordingly.

So anger creates a public relations problem. You must show those complex sides of your inner self that are overshadowed by your anger. The thing to do is to talk more about your feelings, to tell more about how you see things and what you experience. You need to reveal the complexities of your mind and heart before they are translated into simple anger. You may feel inferior, insecure, overly responsible, worried, untrusting, lonely, unloved, unworthy, or any of a wide range of understandable feelings. Talk about them. You will appear more real and much more sympathetic when you do, and more fully human.

When Angela is ignored or belittled by Chuck, she wants to fly back at him, and she finds it hard to share anything about herself that would make her seem vulnerable to him. But she wants a change, and she works on a plan. The next time Chuck snipes at her, she says something unexpected: "I feel confused when you say that. Sometimes I feel that you really love me and care about me, but when you call something I say stupid, I am stunned, shocked. It shakes my confidence. I'm not sure you know how much I count on you for your approval."

So far, she has talked about her own experience, avoiding accusation and being as complimentary as possible. In her next step she involves him in the conversation. "Maybe you don't know how hurt I feel when you criticize me like that. Can you see how I feel?" A yes answer would mean he understands, and a no would invite her to explain more. Greater awareness of her feelings invites him to be more considerate in what he is doing.

Her statements are the by-now-familiar "I feel" messages, used here to present a more sympathetic picture of your problem. We may use them to show something of our inner humanity, which would otherwise be unobservable.

In my own marriage, I have learned the hard way how important it is to show feelings free from anger. I spent many years getting annoyed at my wife for not seeming to understand my feelings, then finding myself feeling ignored and furious as we sank further into the pattern. The more I explained myself to her, the less she seemed to understand who I really was. I usually present myself clearly, so garbled communication was not the problem. I felt she was intentionally shutting me out and refusing to listen, which made me angrier. It is clear to me now what was happening. My ordinarily calm voice became laced with accusation and anger, and Nancy responded not to my concerns but to the force of my anger. I *felt* rejected and hurt, but I *seemed* mean to her. Is that not the usual problem with being angry? You feel wronged and hurt, but you seem hostile.

When I learned to calm my anger and be considerate of her when I speak, I found that she can be wonderfully responsive to what I say. Any sensitive subject must be communicated in a sensitive way.

When you talk about your own troublesome feelings without blame or accusation, you occasionally recognize the feelings themselves as your own problem, and not merely something your mate did to you. If you look for a way to resolve your feelings on your own, you are better off for it. Perhaps you are annoyed by the way your husband tells jokes because that was how your father told jokes, and it brings up unpleasant memories. Gaining insight into your own feelings may be the only way to alter them.

Some people find it particularly hard to be open about themselves when they are angry because it makes them feel vulnerable. Anger makes them want to look strong, protected, and maybe intimidating, but talking about feelings shows their weaker and more troubled side. This is the whole point, of course. Talking about feelings invites your mate to feel concerned about your predicament instead of about fending off your anger. That is an improvement in itself and a step to something more.

Request What You Want. It is important to move from making a clear statement of your objections to making a clear statement of your preferences. Too many of us focus only on what we do not want, assuming that it is obvious what we do want in its stead. But few people are mind-readers, even in the best of circumstances. And when we are squabbling, our listeners seem to acquire a truly remarkable capacity to avoid the most obvious implications.

Angela might ask Chuck to identify the times he belittled her before her friends so he could try to avoid doing so again. In this case, she is requesting not that he do something but that he avoid doing something, which is more difficult. A critical remark can just slip out along the way while he is talking about something else. You will have better results if you can put the request in a positive form, so that you ask someone to do something rather than to try to not do something.

If you want someone to avoid doing a particular action, ask him to do something that runs contrary to it. In this case, Angela should ask Chuck to compliment her once or twice during an evening when they have friends over. A compliment is something he can actually provide if he wishes and if he puts his mind to it. She could even suggest one or two, if he could not think of any. Mulling over a few compliments and then stating them aloud tends to create a friendlier atmosphere, so that he would be less likely to belittle her. Accentuate something positive, for doing so lessens the negative.

Here as anywhere else, a sweetener can help. Can you mention anything positive that could follow from your request? At the minimum, if someone does what you want, then you will stop growling at him. That is not much of an incentive. Yet in too many angry relationships, that is the only apparent benefit the partner gets from compliance with a request.

The woman who asks for compliments might say how she feels when her husband says something nice to her. She might have to rely on her imagination here, or a good memory: "I remember that when we were first married," she might say, "I always felt that you were proud to be with me. I felt really close to you and safe. I want to feel that way with you again."

Making a specific request may mean placing your ego on the line, since it can be refused or rejected. Because a complaint accuses but requests nothing, it cannot be rejected, so a complaint affords a subtle safety. Some people complain, but they avoid making requests in order to avoid the slap of being turned down. But making a clear request is an obvious and necessary step. Best to take the chance, then go from there.

Strike a Bargain. Perhaps the most obvious way we can get somebody to comply with our wishes is to make it worth their while.[3] Our obvious question should be, "What can I do for you to make this happen?" We might all be surprised by the answers we get to this.

A husband who gripes that his wife is always late finally asks her what he can do to help her be ready on time. He finds out: She wants him to take up some of the slack with two children when she gets home from work so she can have some time to collect herself and get ready. That seems fair enough—maybe they can strike a deal.

A woman wants her husband to do more with her, and she asks what he might want in exchange. To her surprise and to his as well, he does not know what he wants. She asks if it would help if she made the arrangements and were warmer to him when they are together. He sees she is trying to consider his feelings and is pleasantly surprised.

Bargaining may be the most difficult step in breaking angry patterns. It requires both partners be clear about what they want and that each listen to what the other wants. On those occasions when things do not instantly fall into place—just about always—it requires that they remain firm in their requests but friendly in their attitudes. Bargaining takes time and considerable patience.

Take Time to Plan. Whatever course you take, do plan it out. In the midst of a fire fight, many people feel compelled to say something—*anything*. But words spoken in anger further fuel the fire and prevent a resolution. While you have a right to stand up for yourself, you need not be trapped by the first thing that falls out of your open mouth. Should you recognize that something you said is too hurtful, you might retrieve it with a quick apology ("I didn't mean that. I take it back.")

When we have not yet fully grasped the problem and haven't the vaguest plan for how to resolve it, we do well to go slowly. A simple request for time works magic: "I may have a problem with that, but I'm not sure how I feel about it yet. Give me a few minutes, will you?" Any fight can surely wait a few minutes while you figure out what you want to say.

Many people get caught up in endless arguments because they cannot let the other person have the last word. It is as if their sacred honor hung on every unanswered accusation. Indeed, many fights that begin with a minor gripe turn into fierce battles over nothing more than who does or does not get to have the last word. Actually, little more is at stake here than two raging egos and some foolish pride. Better to suppress that last oh-so-clever comment of yours and leave the argument where it is. Take some time to cool off and think things out.

I see husbands and wives who feel they always get the worst of it but who continue to squawk and squabble anyway. I try to convince them to walk away from it. I do not want to tell them that they are wrong to fight, which would invite resistance, but only that it is not in their best interest. Humor can deliver the message. The following tale is a favorite of mine.

"A bird falls out of its nest, lands in the cold snow, and is about to freeze to death. A Saint Bernard sees the poor fellow and gently takes the bird in his mouth, carries him over to a large and very fresh patty of cow dung, and drops him off there.

"The bird warms up in the dung and is going to be all right. But he smells the stench and chirps loudly in complaint. A fox in the area hears the bird squawk, walks over, sees the little fellow, and eats him."

It is a terrible story, but it has a moral (as you might well expect), which is: "It is not always your enemies that get you there, and it is not always your friends that get you out. But when you are in the crap, keep your mouth shut."[4]

When one partner quits an argument, the other tends to quit as well. It's better to slip away from the heat, cool off, plan where you are going, then warm it up again under circumstances of your own choosing. Your aim is not to charge blindly into the fray but to take charge. Plan out how to get ahead, and you will be better pleased with the results.

If you are not one to shoot your mouth in anger and if your problem is that you tend to keep it shut when you should talk, disregard the advice immediately above. Go on to the next chapter.

8

Passivity, Sulking, and Acquiescence and Outbursts

Passivity is the architect of several varieties of anger patterns. Since expressing anger is often harmful to relationships, most of us have acquired some inhibitions against its free and forceful expression. These inhibitions are sometimes beneficial; they may make us more patient with those we love or more careful in what we say when we get angry. But strict inhibitions can also produce unhappy acquiescence, in which we steam and stew over our injuries rather than taking action to address them. In such cases, our passivity allows our friends and family plenty of leeway to take advantage of us, so that our grievances accumulate until we finally spout off in anger, making matters even worse.

Gender Differences

The current folklore suggests that women, who are considered to be more passive than men, have more difficulty in expressing their anger than men.[1] The argument runs that society considers anger in females to be improper, unfeminine, unladylike, and unattractive to the opposite sex, and that parents and other socialization agents conspire to teach girls that they should never get angry. Presented in popular and feminist writings on anger, this position is easily accepted for its intuitive appeal and for lack of a better alternative.

But is it true? Available research provides conclusions to the contrary.[2]

Does society actually prohibit anger in girls more than in boys? Boys do seem to be rowdier and more aggressive than girls. But it is only about a quarter of the boys who are particularly unruly, while the remaining majority of boys have similar temperaments to the girls'. One cannot assume therefore that society winks at aggression in boys. Society discourages anger and hostility in children regardless of gender. Since boys are more apt to be aggressive, as research shows, parents and teachers are *more* apt to punish boys than girls, and to give harsher punishments and go to greater lengths to control aggression in boys than in girls.

Nor is it true that parents are noticeably concerned that their daughters be passive and unassertive in order to be feminine. Research shows little indication that parents today try to inculcate either boys or girls into "typical masculine" or "stereotypical feminine" role behavior.[3] While parents do try to curtail the appearance of feminine interests in boys lest a boy be a "sissy" or gay, they are seldom upset about the appearance of the more typically male interests in girls. Girls are allowed to be tomboys, which is considered only a stage in their growing up.

Among adults, men do tend to be somewhat more aggressive than women, although the contrast is generally not as great as is often argued. Men are seen to be more aggressive than women in some situations, such as with strangers, but not necessarily among friends or family. Nor can it be concluded that men are more comfortable in expressing their anger. Men generally appear to be just as likely to hold it in when they are angry as women are. If a woman stifles her anger at an obnoxious supervisor for fear of being fired, a man in the same situation is likely to have very much the same fears and do much the same thing. Men and women both struggle to suppress their anger in job situations, where the penalties for hostile outbursts are severe.[4]

A study of some eighty men and women tracked their ordinary activities over a week and found no differences between them in the amount of anger they experienced.[5] The men and women expressed their anger in similar ways, verbally in most instances; only a few hit, slapped, or threw things. In contrast to the usual stereotype of women as feeling more guilt over their angry outbursts, the men were as likely as the women to feel irritable, gloomy, ashamed, or guilty after an outburst. The study found that women were more apt to cry when they were angry than men and were more likely to withhold customary benefits, such as participation in sexual relations.

Simply by listening to how often men and women talk angrily about their mates, one could easily conclude that women are generally angrier at men than the other way around. Women tend to complain more openly to friends and acquaintances, rehashing their alleged mistreatments and airing their grievances about their mates.[6] But expressing anger more frequently to friends does not mean that women are angrier—only that they talk more openly about it when they are angry. Women are simply freer in expressing anger and other feelings than men are. Men are angry just as often, but they are not as likely to talk about it. Making complaints about being mistreated by a wife or girlfriend, they seem to feel, would belie the image of masculine strength.

So when anger arises, we ought to recognize that it is simply not true that women will stew over it while men will be freer in expressing it. A man is at least as likely to stifle his anger toward a woman as the other way around. In spite of its decidedly unmanly flavor, men are just as likely as women to sulk or to resist passively rather than fight openly.

Let's look now at how inhibitions against anger mold and perpetuate its expression.

Sulking

Here is a commonplace incident of sulking that is a passive expression of anger. While his wife attends her church group, Samuel finds himself alone for the evening to fend for himself and take care of their two small children. It does not seem like much for her to ask of him, but he is unhappy about it. He feels uncomfortable being tethered to the household, and he is lonely and feels out of place managing children too young to provide real companionship. Since he travels on business and is away from home more than she, he cannot legitimately complain about her having an evening out on her own. And surely a man is supposed to be competent and self-sufficient enough to manage the family for a few hours without his wife around. But Sheila seems to work late often, and she goes to school meetings and spends time with her friends. So he feels at loose ends, but more than that. He feels that she is inconsiderate of him and insensitive to the bonds of their marriage. While he may not want to state it so bluntly, he feels abandoned, unloved, and mistreated by her. He is not sure he has the right to feel that way, but he is angry nonetheless.

What does he do about it? Samuel cannot tell his wife that he is troubled by her leaving, lest he reveal a weakness, and he does not feel that he would be justified anyway in asking her to stay in every night. So an open complaint is not an option for him. His anger, in combination with his inhibition against its expression, places him in a bind. He finds no productive resolution. As an answer to his impossible situation, he sulks.

Sulking itself is a peculiar activity in that it involves no special activity at all. It can be done anywhere, along with almost anything else. One can sulk at work or at play, while cooking a meal or waiting for someone to finish eating. One can sulk in the midst of sexual relations or while refusing to get involved in them. Sulking can be the sound of banging pans and slamming doors or the heavy quiet of an unspoken complaint.

Sulking is generally characterized by the absence of an otherwise typical activity. A sulker is uncooperative, uninvolved, as slow as sin, and ever so uncommunicative as to what is going on. A sulker does not talk to you, or look at you, or seem to want to be around you.

Inside this broad lethargy is an aura of sullenness and anger and a sense that the sulker blames you for the impossibility of his life. Sulking is often best identified by this murky atmosphere of anger. If you are close to a sulker, you can feel something invisibly striking out at you. But a sulker is also genuinely hurt, and conveys a sense of agony and pain alongside the murky resentment.

We think of sulking as something that other people do, not that we do, and understandably so. Few people admit to sulking, and then only later, in retrospect, not at the time of its occurrence. Samuel surely would not want to admit that he is sulking. Sulking is a camouflaged expression of anger, undertaken when one is unwilling to express the anger openly. To admit to sulking would be to unravel the camouflage and reveal the unacceptable anger that lies underneath it.

Typically, people sulk when they are seriously angered but are inhibited from openly expressing their anger. The grievance may appear petty and unworthy, or they may hold little hope of resolving the problem openly. They may also be unwilling to state the grievance for fear of appearing weak or immature.

A husband whose wife refuses sexual relations with him may feel deeply injured by her refusal, but hide his hurt to conceal his vulnerability and maintain his manhood. His complaints cannot force her to desire him sexually, but he feels trapped in his commitment to her. So in the ancient and honorable tradition of high-schoolers whose amorous advances meet with rejection, he sulks.

In another instance, a young wife looks forward to getting flowers on Valentine's Day but is hurt when her husband forgets the day altogether. Yet she does not tell him what he did wrong, nor does she tell him ahead of time what she expects. She has complained before about not receiving flowers, but what did it get her? If she made an open complaint again, it would only be ignored again, which would hurt her feelings more. And it would appear petty for her to be so upset over a few flowers. Anyway, since he is not considerate at all of her, why should she make it easy on him? Refusing to tell him what is wrong, she leaves it to him to figure out on his own. And if he squirms a bit until he does, that is fine with her.

Sulking is common to both genders, although the issues involved vary. It may be called "pouting" when a female does it, which is the same thing under another label. Sulking begins as the tactic a child uses in response to an overpowering parent, and it continues as the ploy of one who feels weak against an apparently stronger adversary. Men who sulk veer farther from their expected roles than do women, since nothing so belies the masculine ideal of independence and strength in a relationship as hapless sulking against the apparent power of a woman. But that does not mean men avoid doing it. Rather, men are less likely to admit to it when they do sulk.

One who cannot acknowledge sulking cannot acknowledge its aims, but it has a purpose nonetheless. Like other acts of anger, sulking aims to punish, to force concessions, and to even the tally.

Sulking is not a failure to express anger—sulking *is* an expression of anger. Its tiresome silence merely serves to obscure its aims and to avoid an open fight.

Sulking itself perpetuates the very inhibitions that prevent the open expression of anger. One who sulks is nevertheless so consumed by rage that he naturally concludes it would do great harm were he to ever be careless enough to release it. The longer he sulks, the more he fears his own anger and the less inclined he is to talk openly about what is wrong.

More than other forms of anger, sulking is particularly clumsy in accomplishing its objectives. A more miserable tactic would be hard to imagine. Contrast sulking to a martial arts discipline, such as judo. In judo, you apply your full force in a brief but strategic motion, to gain the maximum amount of leverage against your opponent. Sulking, by contrast, expends your power over a seemingly interminable span of time, carelessly, and gains little advantage or none at all. Sulking is a form of combat, but one perhaps more undisciplined than any you might imagine.

Sulking is likely to gain the sulker only minimal advantages. It seems to be more effective in preventing something from being done than in eliciting something that one wants. Thus, since her husband sulks when she goes out at night, Sheila might give up and stay home, figuring the time away is not worth the consequences when she returns home. But she is not inclined to be more involved with Samuel or more affectionate, if that is what he really wants. A persistent sulk may hobble an opponent, but it invites contempt rather than love, and it provokes stubborn resistance rather than cooperation.

While sulking may serve to get back at someone, it can hardly serve to get even. The one who sends the telegram must pay too high a price for its delivery. The interpersonal message of the sulker is, "Look how miserable you have made me feel, you jerk!" Yet the unhappiness is not just a pretense but is genuinely experienced. Samuel is not just pretending to be hurt, as if it were a shallow game. Sullen and withdrawn, stewing over his predicament, his pain is genuine. But since he continues to blame Sheila for his misery, he comes no closer to evening the score no matter how long he sulks.

In addition to causing turmoil in a relationship, sulking perpetuates itself by broadening the sense of grievance that provokes it in the first place. Troubled as he dwells on his grievance, Samuel blames Sheila for the continuing pain he experiences. She tries to console him, asks what is wrong, and assures him that she does care for him. But he shuns her attentions, as one invariably does in the midst of a major sulk. He will not be cheered up and will not let go and behave as if nothing were wrong. Sulkers do not budge easily. So his pain and sense of mistreatment continues, longer and more severely than it would have if he were not sulking.

Like others who sulk, Samuel cannot distinguish between the hurt caused by what his wife does and the hurt caused by his own sullen response to it. The whole unpleasant experience blends together, and what might have been minor inconvenience becomes a major incident that stands between them. He holds her to blame for the miserable experience he was forced to endure while sulking over how unfairly she neglected him.

The perceived injury justifies the sulking, but the longer one sulks the more injured one feels. So sulking justifies itself, as the sense of injury one experiences while sulking justifies further sulking. The pattern perpetuates itself (figure 8–1).

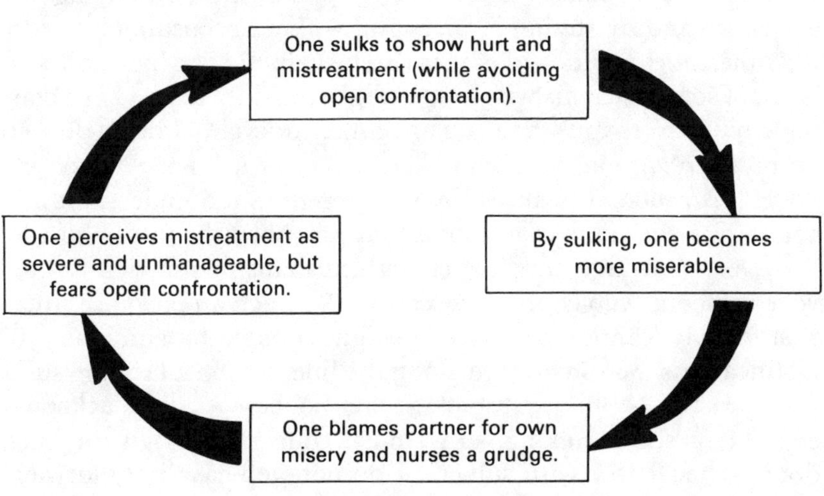

Figure 8–1. Sulking

Any spell of sulking eventually subsides as the sulker gains some satisfaction from it or it just wears out. But the perception of having been injured remains, as does the sense of powerlessness to do anything constructive about it. So at the next provocation, the person is just as likely to sulk again, or more likely, since the grievances accumulate and his backlog of old injuries is now longer.

Clearing the Air. How do we break the pattern? It is the partner who sulks who controls the action, not the partner who faces it. Sulking is so self-centered and self-contained that it is not easily subdued by a sympathetic spouse. Reassurances are wasted, apologies are awkward, and conversation is met with silence punctuated by short bites of sarcasm. Sometimes the partner's best approach is to be patient, stay calm, and avoid doing anything to aggravate the situation. Go about your business and wait for the storm to blow over on its own. But no method is foolproof. A sulker may interpret his partner's calm as aloofness or lack of concern ("So you're avoiding me!") and continue the sullenness until he provokes a confrontation. Only then does it all blow over—until the next unavoidable mishap.

It is the one who sulks who must alter the pattern. And the pattern can be changed with what appears to be only a minimum of insight. The sulker can begin by openly acknowledging his grievance and by stating it fairly and without accusation. The "I feel" messages mentioned earlier can be helpful. The husband who is out of sorts when his wife leaves might consider telling her about it: "I really miss you when you are gone," or even, "I don't do well on my own without you." So what if it's not macho? At least it's honest. A problem so stated invites closeness and understanding, countering the sense of isolation that provoked the initial hurt.

Every marriage contains enough mishaps to sufficiently provoke someone who is predisposed to sulk. Such an intimate situation simply cannot be made benign enough to eliminate all justifications. So somewhere along the line, we must face the sulking head on. An initial obstacle is that nobody wants to acknowledge he or she is sulking, so we must come in through the back door. When I talk with sulkers, I do not step cavalierly forward and tell them that they are sulking. That would be perceived as an accusation. Instead, I simply talk to them about how they feel and what they are trying to do about it. I legitimize everything, showing that it makes sense for them to do exactly what they are doing. Once people see that they make sense, once their plan is fully conscious, they can see that their tactic is headed for certain failure. If I mention sulking at all, it is only in passing, to help fill in the picture.

With Samuel, I legitimize his feelings: "It matters to you that Sheila be at home with the family in the evenings, and it seems she is gone too much whenever she pleases, without really caring about how it affects you. You do not appreciate it, and it seems reasonable to make that known. So when she comes home, you are distant from her and uninvolved. You seem to be saying, 'Look how bad you made me feel.' And it seems you have every right to let her know how she makes you feel."

Then, to familiarize him with his own position, I invite him to participate: "Try saying aloud to your wife, 'I am withdrawn from you and miserable to show you how much you have injured me.' "

He does not want to say that. Samuel is not sure that is what he really means, he says, and it feels awkward—naturally. No one is eager to acknowledge something that appears so foolish. I loosen the rope a little, then persist. "It may not be exactly right," I concede, "but for now we are just exploring. Try it out, just to see how it feels when you say it." So he does. And when he says it, he steps into the uncomfortable truth: He realizes that sulking is exactly what he is doing.

I try to make it easier to swallow. "We all do some of that sometimes. I do it, most people I know do it. And sometimes for good reason. The important thing is to see it, to acknowledge it to yourself. And once you acknowledge it, you are well on your way to resolving it."

Consciousness does indeed curtail sulking, for its underhandedness requires a cloak of confusion. You cannot admit that you are acting miserable in order to show your partner how much she hurt you, but continue to believe nonetheless that you are miserable simply because she hurt you so much. Once you recognize that you are a willful participant, you see your own responsibility in the matter—and your own folly. You realize that you are making yourself miserable to send a message. And when you see that it is foolish, you stop—at least for the moment. As long as you are conscious of its purpose, the sulking vanishes.

Unfortunately, this insight is usually transitory. As soon as you lose sight of its purpose, sulking reappears. So it is important to write down your insight and to review it several times a day over the first several weeks. Push yourself to talk about it to your spouse or to a friend. Nothing makes us quite so aware of our own actions as having to acknowledge them aloud to a companion.

Sulking can be overcome by those who acknowledge it. It may be difficult for you to acknowledge to yourself that you are making yourself miserable to send someone a message. It is still more difficult to acknowledge it to the person who you feel has wronged you. Yet it is well worth a try, and you may be pleased with the results.

Acquiescence and Outbursts

Since too much conflict is rough on the spirit, many of us choose to ignore or slough off minor aggravations rather than to do battle over them. Although we are willing to pay a small price for the peace and comfort of getting along, the total price may be higher than we figured. Grievances multiply when unaddressed, so that anger builds to an uncontrollable fury, then bursts loose in a torrent of accusations with unproductive and sometimes devastating consequences. Sometime later, the concerns still unresolved, the combatants tire of the fight, simmer down, and call a truce. Fear of another ugly incident suppresses any further mention of the grievances, until anger builds to the next uncontrolled explosion. Moods swing between unproductive acquiescence and unproductive rage. At the heart of this pattern is a failure to confront troubles early on, when cooler heads might still splice together an acceptable compromise.

Mary's husband Charles is an avid television sports fan during the football, basketball, and baseball seasons, and he has an intermittent interest in golf and tennis. So in the evenings and on weekends, she is left with the housework (which she does not usually mind), the children (who do not usually mind her), and no companionship (which she does mind but believes should not bother her so much). It does seem fair for her to manage the home front now and then so that he can enjoy a favorite broadcast. But the "now and then" has expanded to several nights a week and most weekends, transforming her into a sports widow.

Mary finds herself stewing about it. She is not sure what to say to Charles, and she does not want to be a complainer and a bad sport all the time. She wonders if a better wife or a better adjusted one would simply adapt and get along with it the way it is. Many women surely have it worse, she realizes. Yet she is not happy, and it seems unfair that he does just what he wants. Her resentment builds. She says something to him and asks him for more time. He wants to be more available, he agrees, but nothing changes. A basketball classic is on, and his attention is glued to the screen. Not wanting to nag, she lets it slide. Her resentment builds further.

Finally, steaming, Mary lets him have it. Unable to speak up for herself when she is calm and rational, she allows her anger to speak for her. She yells, she cries. She accuses him of tuning her out and of rechanneling all his love from her to the television. He is speechless—which is just as well, as she is too angry to listen to him anyway. Finally, her fury spent, she quits the confrontation and goes off to be by herself and regain her composure. Nothing is resolved, of course, nor could it be resolved that way. She has said more than she wanted to say, feels hurt that he gave her no reassurances, and is hurt that she created further distance between them. She feels foolish, confused, and afraid of the bitterness that now is between them. She hopes they can patch up their differences, settle in, and get along again. This sort of outburst is obviously no answer. She will try to adjust to his interests rather than go through all that again. So she is subdued for the moment. But her resentments will build again, and the pattern will repeat. While she does not believe she has the right to tell her husband what to do, she is free enough to complain when he does not do as she wishes.

Anger controls and shapes the way complaints are handled. Generally cautious and compliant, Mary works to control herself to avoid unnecessary quarrels. Only when her anger gets the best of her does she lash out, but then it seems that it is not her own will but the anger that is doing the talking. And in some ways, it is. Only when she is angry does she feel she has the right to confront him—otherwise, she is too concerned about being pushy or selfish. So she says in anger what she would not say otherwise. And what she says in anger is more alarming than what she should or would want to say were she in control of herself. While she should see that she has a right to state her case, she would want to do it calmly and with less venom. Anger tends to raise the stakes, promoting a simple complaint into an all-out attack. And the greater the anger, the more punishing the attack. The harsher the attack, of course, the less the likelihood of a mutually agreeable outcome.

Mary's bind is that she acquiesces until she is too angry to control herself, but by then the anger that argues for her is so unruly that it makes a bigger mess of things. She is characteristically moody, vacillating between passive acceptance—with its understandable resentment—and uncontrolled outbursts—with their unhappy consequences inviting remorse and further passivity. The pattern perpetuates itself (figure 8–2).

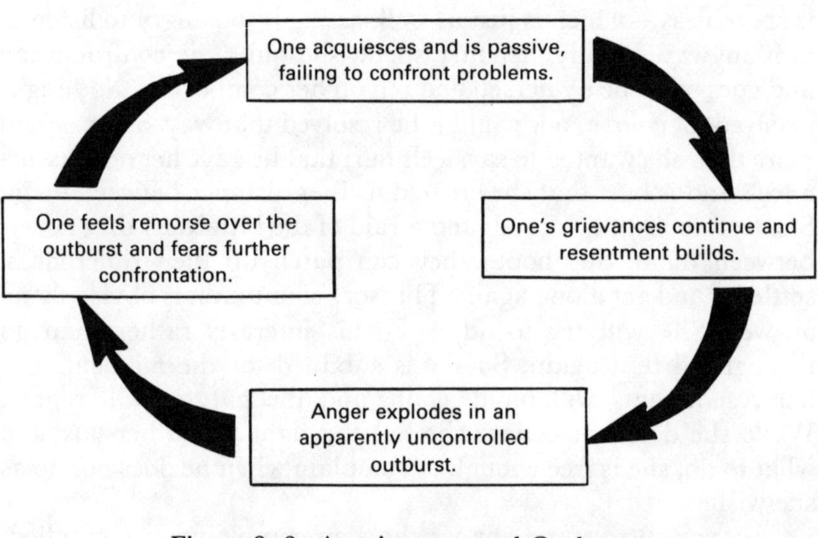
One acquiesces and is passive, failing to confront problems.
One's grievances continue and resentment builds.
Anger explodes in an apparently uncontrolled outburst.
One feels remorse over the outburst and fears further confrontation.

Figure 8–2. Acquiescence and Outbursts

℞. To steady these mood swings, we must first recognize the legitimacy of our own grievances. The sports widow must accept that she has a right to prefer her husband to be more available and that she has a right to try to figure out how she might get him to change. She must take the initiative to speak up on her own and not wait for her anger to speak for her. She does not have a guarantee that the first thing she tries is going to be successful. So she must confront it as a challenge, to be perhaps resolved with persistence and several new plans of attack. If the first plan is unsuccessful, she must maintain her right to hold on to her preference and figure out another plan.

A problem presented calmly does not create the sense of remorse afterward that a heated argument creates. So whether Mary gains anything or not, nothing is sacrificed. Nobody gets angry, and she can be pleased with how she handled herself. The atmosphere remains comfortable, and the spirit remains to try again.

She chooses a time when he is between games and says she has a question for him. Charles asks what it is. She says that she knows she is an interesting person, if nothing else because she finds life interesting. And then she pops the question: "I want to know what would make me just as interesting as the golf classic that you were watching this afternoon." Caught by surprise, he has no idea how to respond. "Well," she pushes, "think about it. Because I am ready to try something. I really do want to see more of you, and I may be ready for an adventure." It gets him thinking.

But does anything change? Probably not at the time. A comment such as hers is just a beginning. The beauty of it is that she begins a dialogue without having to sacrifice goodwill to do it. She can feel satisfied with herself for making a beginning, and confident that the next step can be taken without an unmanageable blow-out.

The moment of our hottest anger is a poor time to speak out, but some time must count as the right time. After our anger subsides, our temptation is to welcome the calm and to turn our attention to pleasanter things. Most of us do not change our bearings and willfully sail into another storm, but that is exactly what we must do. The sports widow whose anger has recently cooled must realize that the problem still remains. She should use this time wisely, to chart a bold course that will sail her back into a confrontation with the old problem.

While it might be preferable to speak up sooner, before you get really angry, in many situations you find yourself unprepared to do so. You may not fully understand what is going wrong and may need time to think about it. You may not know what you would want to say. No matter. The typical problem is no crisis, and time is on your side. Take as long as you need to figure it out, then jump back in with what you really want to say. But be sure that as long as an opportunity remains, you do get back to it.

Anger and Depression. Close companions, depression and anger play against each other as they plague the unlucky individual. There is a causal link between sulking and depression; besides mulling over grievances, sulking involves lethargy and inner pain, the mainstays of depression. One who is prone to sulk is already well on his way to having troublesome bouts of depression. The man who sulks when his wife leaves for the evening is not a happy camper. Cold to the normal satisfactions of being a husband and father, he is likely to be forlorn and depressed.

The sense of powerlessness and futility that contribute to sulking contribute to depression in other ways as well. The sports widow who has the confidence to push for something better is more likely to be spirited and active than melancholic. A good surge of righteous anger can be invigorating. But her optimism will not survive too many losing battles; when the angry confrontation goes sour, she feels remorse over the injury she inflicted and a sense of futility over her fate in the marriage. Her incompatibility with her husband remains, but it is accompanied now by a feeling of guilt over the pain she inflicted and feelings that she is a nag who deserves no better. Her battle lost and her spirit broken, she succumbs to her circumstances for want of a better alternative. She sees her marriage not as a choice but as an unpleasant compromise with a brick wall. As long as she perceives that she must buckle under to the unacceptable situation, she is likely to experience depression.

Mary will alternate between spells of depression and outbursts of anger as long as her marital conflict remains unresolved. More angry confrontations further jeopardize her marriage, bringing apprehension, guilt, further inhibitions, and depression. Then the tensions burst forth in more anger. Her mood swings from justified outbursts of anger to acquiescence and depression. The pattern perpetuates itself.

As with the other acquiescence and outburst patterns, one must be careful to challenge these problems thoughtfully, in a way that is likely to resolve the problem rather than make it worse. Taking action is especially important because one who is depressed is inclined to let things slide most of the time when no immediate action is required. Those who tumble between depression and anger need support in overcoming their gooey combination of marital chaos and inner turmoil.

Generosity and Anger. Some partners continue doing and overdoing for their apparently ungrateful spouses, rage briefly over being taken for granted, then continue doing and overdoing. Their conduct swings between caretaking and griping, but nothing really changes.

Ginger, a young and hard-working superwife, feels compelled to do absolutely everything in her power to make her marriage successful. She does the laundry, the housecleaning, and the shopping, and she holds down a good job outside the home. She manages the meals, too, but these are not your ordinary workaday fast-food take-home meals or a few things warmed up and thrown together. She has higher standards than that. She prepares soup, salad, and several separate dishes coordinated to arrive hot at the same time, followed by a dessert. On weekends she makes gourmet entrees as well, expanding by several hours the time needed to prepare the food.

Ginger does not mind the cooking, but she wants it to be special to her husband, Joshua. But it is not. Used to the woman being the homemaker and not himself a gourmet, he takes it all for granted. He eats whatever she fixes, but will not compliment her on his own and cannot be coaxed into doing so. So she feels unappreciated and used, like an ordinary housemaid but without pay or fringe benefits. Her patience and good cheer wear thin, and she becomes frazzled and resentful. She gets upset with him and gripes and complains, but she might as well be yelling at the walls for all the good it does. He takes things for granted, and a few harsh words are not going to change his stripes. He says he does not know what to say to her. He would be more contented with her were she less compulsive about the housekeeping and meals and in a better mood more of the time.

Ginger's rage changes quickly to insecurity and remorse, as she worries that her outbursts are too harsh. Wanting his appreciation and feeling she has to somehow make it up to him, she resumes her caretaker responsibilities. By being a better wife, she figures, perhaps she can again merit his love. She continues doing and overdoing for her ungrateful spouse, and the pattern perpetuates itself.

Unless Joshua suddenly changes, which he is not likely to do, Ginger should try to steady her mood swings by pacing herself so that she does a fairer and more reasonable amount of work and has time to be peaceful with herself as well. Many of the routine tasks require cooperation from her husband, and she may have to compromise her own housekeeping standards to allow for an untrained beginner. Since he does not appreciate her meals, she does not have to cook them. She should try to limit her special productions to things he really appreciates.

And she should look more closely at her own motivations as well. Does she truly believe that Joshua will appreciate what she cooks for him? She has seen him take it for granted too many times to believe that. But she continues preparing special meals because she feels it is a good and noble thing to do and because he *ought* to appreciate it. If he does not, she has still done what she thinks she should to be a good wife, and she can blame him for the impasse. She continues overworking to make sure she is right, even though it makes him wrong. She could be nobler by being a little less perfect.

A Balanced Judgment on Anger

The concepts presented above allow us to reconcile several seemingly contradictory viewpoints on anger. The Christian tradition that condemns anger as sinful is troubled by its punishing qualities and the careless injury it can wreak upon a community of love and intimate fellowship. Christian teachings want us to strive to control our anger so that we can look out for others rather than harm them. But the mental health movement observes that anger that is condemned by authorities does not vanish, but is often camouflaged and rechanneled into underhanded forms of aggression that can be quite harmful. Furthermore, health professionals note anger may serve to signal that something is amiss in an important relationship. So therapists advocate that we accept our anger and express it openly, to stand up for ourselves and assert our rights.

There is something important in each of these positions. Anger does indeed act to punish, and we would do well to decide carefully when and how we do battle with so potent a weapon. But condemning anger does not necessarily calm it, and we would do better to try to understand its workings and resolve the situations that provoke it. Anger is normal and natural, and we must learn to be gentle with ourselves and accept the legitimacy of our feelings when we get angry.

Is it important to express our anger? That depends on how we are inclined to express it. Anger might be expressed by pouting, by slamming doors, or by yelling profanities; the costs of such expressions surely outweigh any expected benefits. The question as stated is too ambiguous, and we should reformulate it. Ask instead, is it good to state our position? The answer is an unambiguous yes. It is important to express our grievances, so that we can begin to understand each other and to negotiate our differences. Perceiving that we are mistreated evokes anger in us, and resolving the mistreatment is the most obvious way to calm the anger. So if "express your anger" means "clarify your grievances," then yes, it is indeed important to do that.

Splice it all together, and out comes a small patchwork of simple truisms:

- Accept your anger, but be careful what you do with it
- Confront the situations that make you angry, but do so fairly and with as little anger as possible

Anger is an overzealous ally, propelling us to stand up for our rights but prone to excess, often causing more trouble than it is worth. So when you roll up your sleeves and take on your beloved adversary, try to create a little less heat and a little more light.

Part IV

The Mix and Mismatch of Sexual Interests

In the romantic beginnings of a relationship, our infatuation commands our interest and carries us along. In that sweet version of altered reality called "being in love," we find ourselves yearning, fantasizing, frequently aroused, and easily pleased at being with our beloved. We see this rush of emotion as the natural response to our sweetheart, arising on its own and requiring no work or special attention to generate it. When love is new, it is all spontaneous and natural. The ready sexual attraction is one of the hallmarks of the romantic phase of a relationship.

Most people who are together in love wish it would last forever. Many people expect it to continue forever, and a few bet the farm on it (and their marriages as well). Unfortunately but inevitably, the magic does subside. The romantic phase can last up to a year or so after marriage, by some estimates.[1] In one study husbands and wives reported that they became less romantic and less satisfied with the quality of their relationship over the first fifteen months of marriage.[2] Most would not say they became unhappy—only less euphoric. So somewhere within this span of time the rush subsides, leaving us becalmed on our own in the unforeseen settledness of a lifelong commitment. Sometime after the honeymoon, we recognize the limitations. We may wonder what caused us to be so insanely attracted to this ordinary individual who is now our spouse.

When the infatuation runs out or if we were not so romantic initially, we must look for new ways to love. When the attraction is no longer so strong, we need to learn to cultivate it. The following chapters investigate sexual interest and the lack thereof in matured relationships. They focus not on the act of sex itself but on how two sets of sexual interests match or mismatch in the broader context of a relationship. Sexuality is viewed not as merely a biological process, but as a way of relating to each other. The rich fulfillment of sexuality comes not merely from the neural stimulation to orgasm (which many late adolescents can accomplish on their own) but from the affirmation that we are loved, appreciated, wanted, and cherished, and that our wishes are genuinely considered, intensified by the openness and passion of the meeting. But while sex is typically seen as a vehicle for gaining pleasure, to be practiced and perfected, it is much more than that. Sex is about attraction, bonding, commitment; it is about power and subjugation, success and failure, acceptance and rejection; it is about fairness and balancing the score; it is about pride, insecurity, and most of the other undercurrents of intimate relationships.

9

Imbalanced Sexual Interests

"How often do you have sex?" asks the psychiatrist.
"Hardly ever," the man replies. "Three times a week."
At the same time in another office, her therapist poses the same question.
"All the time," she replies. "Three times a week."
—Woody Allen and Diane Keaton in *Annie Hall*.

One partner wants sex more frequently, for longer periods of time, and with greater variety, while the other wants it less frequently and feels safer with the familiar. Neither is satisfied. The one who wants it more feels continually rejected, unloved, and sexually unfulfilled, while the one who wants it less feels continually pressured, unloved, and sexually inadequate.

When we consider sexual problems, the sexual malfunctions of individuals tend to come to mind. We think of inhibited sexual interest, frigidity, premature ejaculation, or impotence, which are problems of failed performance; or satyriasis or nymphomania, which are problems of too much performance. But these are not strictly individual problems, as much rides on the match between the partners. Neither inhibited interest nor unusually high interest is necessarily a problem if the partner is compatible. Those with minimal sexual interest match well enough with like-minded partners, and those with heightened libidos may thrive with a mate with similar inclinations. It is the imbalance in sexual interest between partners that spells sure trouble for two individuals who must accommodate themselves to the same bed.

Imbalanced sexual interest is a common troublemaker in many marriages. It is one of the more frequent complaints that marriage therapists and sex therapists hear, and it appears to be prevalent in many otherwise satisfactory marriages.[1] Indeed, it seems to be the unusual pair who after several years of marriage still have similar levels of sexual interest in each other.

Our modern permissive society has come a long way from the traditional morality of yesteryear, which condemned sexually active men and women for succumbing to what was then considered the baser and more primitive side of human nature. Society now assumes that those with low or nil sexual interest are unhealthily inhibited from natural and normal sexuality. Mainstream sex therapists tend to see imbalances in sexual interest as an inhibited sexual responsiveness on the part of the less interested partner. Treatment seeks to increase the lower responsiveness to match that of the more interested partner.[2] Even those who would not want to argue that more sex is better sex might nonetheless judge that less is probably worse.

Sex and marriage therapists might focus more profitably on the different levels of desire and on the interactions between the partners.[3] Only seen in the context of the relationship can sexual interest problems show their true colors.

Gender Differences. Normal differences between men and women contribute to sexual imbalances. The following synopsis, drawn from the work of Kinsey, Masters and Johnson, and a summary by Kaplan and Sager, portrays average or typical patterns at various ages.[4] Since individuals vary widely from these averages, these generalizations are meant only to provide a basis for comparisons.

Imbalanced sexual interest is obvious among adolescents, so obvious that it is a wonder that the youngsters at that age get along together at all. When teenage boys and girls do get together, they are miles apart in what they want from each other. Males in later adolescence are sexually overheated, readily aroused by anything and everything. Adolescent boys are turned on by skin that shows and by the clothes that cover it; by the warmth of the true-blue sweetheart and by the coldness of the stone fox; by the fantasies in their minds and by the physical touch at the school dance; and by the wiggles of girls when they walk and by their calmness when they sit very still. Sex is an obsession for teenage boys—intense, urgent, and pervasive. Seeking sexual contact is a preoccupation for them, although sexual release is more usually attained through frequent masturbation. Several orgasms a day are quite typical. Whether teenage boys have the confidence to act on it or the conviction to restrain themselves, the strong sexual impulse is always there. Males reach their peak of sexual steam as youths, at seventeen or eighteen, and from there they experience a slow but continual decline over the decades that follow.

The pattern for females is in important ways the reverse of that of males. Female sexual arousal is slower in youth, and many teenage girls experience little pressure for sexual release through orgasm. Arousal increases through middle age. Since there is more variation among females than among males, generalizations are not as reliable. Some teenage girls are as sexually driven as the boys, providing exceptions to the rule.

Sexual activity among young girls is more often for the romance or for social considerations, than for sex per se. In adolescence, it is usually the fellows who push for sex and the girls who comply or refuse. Some girls have sex within a committed relationship, out of love for the fellow or to hold his interest. Some of the more adventuresome spirits gamble, to impress a boy and capture his interest. Some girls have sex out of loneliness, for the companionship it provides and the temporary sense of intimacy. Many go along with the pressure to have sex simply for lack of a graceful way out.

So among teenagers, boys are generally obsessed with sex, while girls are obsessed with boys. It is from sexual interest that boys seek to overcome their discomfort with girls, while it is often because of romantic interest that girls overcome their qualms and tangle with sex.

The passage of a few years lessens the average sexual imbalance between males and females. Sexual pressure in men subsides when they are in their thirties, and by their forties, orgasms per se are no longer so important and men focus more on the sensual aspects of the experience. In their fifties, many men are absorbed in their vocations and go weeks without having sexual fantasies at all.

Sexual responsiveness in females increases from adolescence and well into their forties. In their thirties, especially after bearing children, women respond faster and more intensely to erotic stimulation, and they seek out and initiate sex more frequently. They may prefer longer lovemaking sessions, and multiple orgasms are common. The thirties and early forties, it seems, is the time when married women are most likely to have extramarital affairs.[5]

Somewhere in their late twenties or early thirties, the average sexual interest is at about the same level in men and women. A few years after that, the average sexual interest is higher for women.

Thus, in adolescence when males are most highly sexed, their counterparts are more cautious and often unavailable, while in the middle and later years when females are most interested, many men their age are "over the hill." This is surely one of the better ironies perpetrated upon us by human nature.

Although sexual interest is imbalanced at both ends, in the middle years the average sexual interests of men and women are close enough for many compatible matches. Since individuals vary widely, with some care we could surely select mates with approximately the same level of interest as our own. But imbalanced sexual interest seems to be more common than might be expected from the averages. The patterns of imbalanced interest established in earlier years perpetuate themselves, while relationships that begin with apparently compatible interest tend to become imbalanced as well.

Imbalances Build

Sexual relationships go through several phases. Typically in the first year or so of a first marriage, sex is frequent, somewhat routine, and almost always at the initiation of the husband. This arrangement is apparently comfortable or convenient enough initially, and it continues until one or both partners tire of it.

Marty seems to be always interested in sex. For the first year of his marriage to Lisa, he was the initiator and she was always willing.

While Lisa liked the attention at first, too much of a good thing loses its charm. Something that is always available is easily taken for granted and is no romantic challenge.

Marty's high interest turned gradually into unwanted pressure for sex. He absolutely insisted a few times when she did not want to, and his interest became annoying to her rather than flattering. Now he finds she is frequently uninterested. He feels injured and withdraws from her to sulk quietly about his misfortune. Doing so adds pressure on her, because to refuse him again would be to hurt his pride and ruin his day. But the pressure smothers her fantasies and steals her sense of having a choice in the matter. Having sex becomes just another chore for her, like doing the laundry, to be performed as quickly as possible and have finished.

Marty wants his wife to respond passionately, rather than merely go along with sex, which further increases his pressure on her. Lisa would be more comfortable with sex if she were not expected to attain the height of passion every time.

Growing annoyed by the pressure, Lisa begins to withhold as a way to assert her independence and fight back. He gets the signal, but he misinterprets the message. In turn, he initiates sex more frequently and continues intercourse for longer spans, trying by brute persistence to bring forth the passion he wants from her. But the more Marty pushes, the less passion Lisa has, and the less she has, the more he pushes for it.

Lisa is using unresponsiveness as a way to subdue his overresponsiveness. Experience has taught her that her own passions do indeed arouse him, stimulating him to greater sexual acrobatics and additional requests for more and better sex. So the more she does, it seems, the more he wants from her. Occasionally she breaks the nights-only schedule and agrees to have sex in the morning as well. Then the following morning he wants a repeat of this new and more liberal allowance. She is not ready to have sex *every* morning. She concludes it is better not to begin anything that will raise unwanted expectations.

While Marty wants her to be passionate, he is not easily contented when she does respond to him. He has felt unwanted by her for too long, and when she does want him, it arouses him further. He knows what sex can be like, and he wants it that way again. Inadvertently, he shows that when she shows interest, it only incites him further. Unwittingly, he gives her the very message he wants to avoid.

No matter how much she tries, Lisa figures, her husband will only want more, and she can never satisfy him. To avoid arousing further expectations, she becomes routine in her scheduling and pedestrian in her lovemaking. It is more than coincidence that she seems to avoid doing the things that really would turn him on.

Marty finds he has to push in order to maintain any sexual relationship with her at all. If he did not, he figures, nothing would ever happen. He tries going several days without mentioning sex, which only confirms his conclusion. Lisa appreciates the reprieve and makes no mention of sex. Inadvertently, she shows him that without his pressure, there would be no sex.

He feels rejected and cheated of the passion she could give him, and she feels that she is being used to relieve an insatiable sexual appetite. Neither is pleased by the arrangement, and each blames the other for it. As their satisfactions lessen and their anger increases, their arguments are frequent and their bedroom becomes a battleground. "You are never interested in sex!" he contends, overlooking the good times when she was interested. "You are never interested in anything but sex!" she counters, overlooking any indication to the contrary. The force of one accusation provides the provocation for a counteraccusation, and so on.

Marty argues that their sexual relationship is truly inadequate, in order to support his argument for more sex. He becomes a captive of his own viewpoint and overlooks what Lisa does do for him. And Lisa claims that sex is a burden for her, in order to support her argument for less sex. So she fails to see the pleasures that might otherwise be there for her. Both become victims of their own propaganda.

Sex involves vulnerability, so that the presence of anger and insensitivity make it particularly unsafe for either partner: Marty cannot communicate the tender or sensitive side of his sexual feelings for fear of giving Lisa further grounds to attack him. Lisa is afraid to risk the sexual and passionate side of herself with him for fear of his insensitivity or criticism of her.

Sex is by now a hardship for both of them, to be either managed or endured. For Marty, although he continues to push for sex, it is always unsatisfying. He does it to prove himself or to force her to give in to him, in a trial of his manhood against an unwilling adversary, and surely not a comforting pleasure or a sharing of love. And while Lisa concedes to having intercourse, it is to placate him and not for any satisfaction for herself.

As he continues to push and she continues to withhold, the two of them maintain or actually increase their initial imbalance in sexual interest. The pattern perpetuates itself (figure 9–1).

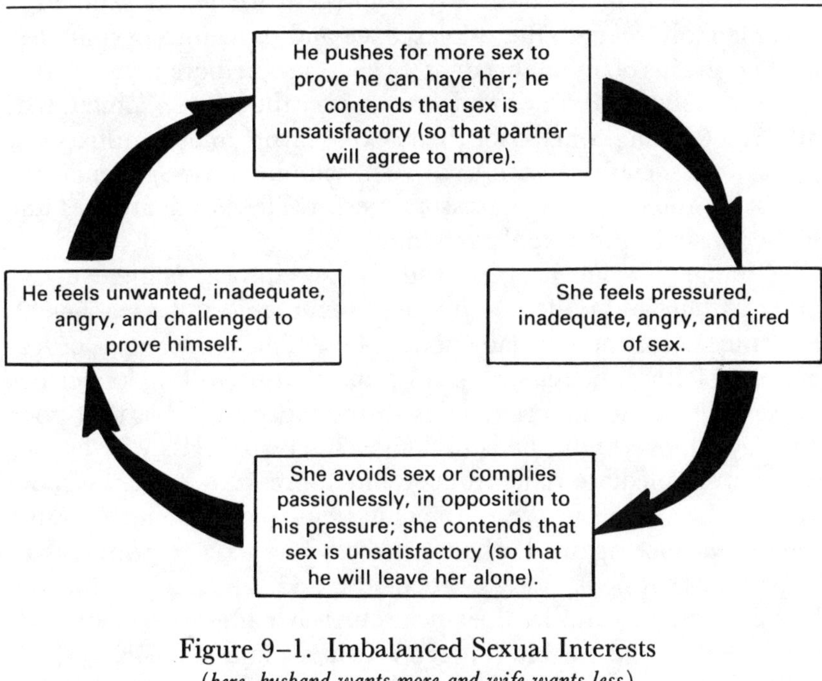

Figure 9–1. Imbalanced Sexual Interests
(here, husband wants more and wife wants less)

An Age of Reversed Imbalances. Nowadays, it is the wife as often as it is the husband who is more interested in having sexual relations, at least after the early years of marriage. In recent surveys, only five percent of wives said that they wished sexual intercourse were less frequent,[6] while fully one-third said that they wished sexual relations were more frequent.[7] This is a marked change from the traditional pattern of years past; in a representative 1920 survey, two-thirds of the wives wanted sex less frequently than their husbands did.[8]

Women who would prefer to have intercourse more often do not necessarily become sexual aggressors and do not typically try to force themselves upon their husbands. More commonly, after making some attempts to ask for more, they remain unsatisfied but are unwilling to push for it and face rejection.

Reversals in the imbalances of youth usually occur gradually over several years, but sometimes they occur quite suddenly. Some reversals follow naturally from the tendency for women to become more sexual after adolescence and of men to become less so. The strains of imbalanced interests can contribute to the changing responsiveness of men and women over the years. Women, who are used to being courted for their sexual favors, may acquire more pleasant associations with sex. Men, who have worn themselves out being the tiresome aggressors, perceive fewer advantages and higher costs in the sexual exchange.

Changes in one partner lead to a reciprocal change in the other. A husband miffed by frequent sexual rejections reaches his tolerance point and has had enough. Out of pride, or anger, or fear of sexual failure, he makes up his mind that he will no longer beg for sex, which he now concludes in retrospect was not that good anyway. So overnight, he is no longer interested. His wife experiences an immediate relief from so much pressure for sex. Gradually, as her own suppressed inclinations recover, she becomes interested once again. Perhaps she sees him as a romantic challenge now that he is more independent, and she pursues him. But he has changed, and he does not return her interest. Their roles are reversed, and the old pattern continues in a new form.

Changes that threaten a marriage can alter the sexual balance suddenly. It is perhaps surprising how many wives who have been uninterested in sex suddenly become aroused when they find out that their husbands are involved in an affair. This increase in sexual interest is for real, not merely a ruse to win back the husband. Feelings of pain and fear and anger are to be expected, but her own awakening sexual interest takes the woman quite by surprise. Perhaps she feels awkward and ashamed at wanting her husband so much now that he is being unfaithful to her. Yet she feels abandoned and afraid when he is away from her, and feels comforted and wanted during the time when they are having sex. Her increased sexual arousal is a natural if sometimes inconvenient yearning for a relationship that she can no longer take for granted. If the situation remains unresolved, her pain and escalating bitterness squelches her surge in sexual interest.

Minor Imbalances Widen. Even relationships that begin with mutual attraction and high sexual compatibility can easily go out of balance. As sexual interest subsides somewhat for one partner, the other may remain attracted and push to maintain the original sexual interest level.

The dynamics involved can cause even small and initially trivial imbalances to snowball into major sexual incompatibilities. Perhaps one night or two, one of the partners is aroused and pushes for sex, while the other is not interested and turns down the invitation. Being out of step now and then is normal and unavoidable. But the one who wants sex even slightly more than the other can feel taken for granted, while the one who wants it slightly less becomes a challenge. So the imbalance increases from there.

Perhaps one of the partners wants to try something new while the other is uncomfortable with it. Perhaps one argues for more oral sex and is accused of being really inconsiderate, while the other argues against it and is accused of being prudish. The impasse becomes the focus of attention, and it flavors the whole sexual relationship.

Sometimes the problem is the timing. One partner wants sex in the morning, the other in the evening; one is worn out while working but wants it continually on vacations, while the other wants it on a more even schedule. It is easy to take sex for granted when it is available, then push for it when it is not to be had.

Unless two partners are wired exactly the same sexually, one will be more interested and the other less interested at some point or another in the relationship. Unless managed carefully and with genuine consideration, even the most mundane imbalances can take on significant proportions.

Rebalancing Sexual Relations

If sexual imbalances were hardwired into human physiology, as many suppose they are, there would be little hope of altering them. We would have to simply continue as our inner programming instructs. But physiology provides only the possibilities—it is attitudes and relationships that shape the output. Relationship changes can strongly affect supposedly ingrained sexual inclinations. The self-perpetuating feature of imbalanced interests suggests that imbalances can be adjusted.

Too many battles over frequency can blind us to the quality of the sexual experiences themselves. In many cases, the basic sexual interests are not nearly as incompatible as they seem. Even partners in extreme cases, where one argues that one *always* wants it and the other *never* gives any, are not necessarily as far apart as they seem. When I ask Marty and Lisa how much each could accept, their answers are surprising. She says she would prefer to have sex once or twice a week but three times might be all right, while he says he would like it every night or more but at least five nights minimum. So these stubborn adversaries are only a one or two count away from a modest compromise at three or four times per week.

To break the pattern, husband and wife must each be willing to accept a compromise. One must be willing to settle for a slightly higher frequency, and the other for a slightly lower frequency than might be preferred. Finding a compromise may be easier than it appears, as any reasonable midpoint is usually an improvement for both of them. The real work of the program is to follow the agreement.

Remember that each partner is bound by his or her particular anxieties. One fears that if he did not push, she would never have sex with him; the other fears that were she more responsive, he would never do anything else. An agreed-upon frequency should provide the needed security for both of them.

Lisa must be willing to promise that they will have sex a minimum number of times per week so that Marty can trust that it will occur without having to push for it. That may not be an easy promise for her to make. Feeling pushed already, she does not feel she should have to promise anything more at all. Any agreement may seem to her merely an acquiescence to his pressures. What if on the assigned night she does not feel like it? Her objections must be considered, but there is an up side for her as well. Making a compromise commitment can remove the continual pressure she feels, and it may be no more than what she is doing unwillingly anyway. One woman I talked with was reluctant to commit herself to having sex with her husband twice a week or to having sex with him at all. Yet over the previous years he had pressured her into having it regularly twice a week or more, but under protest. Her agreeing upon the twice a week would stop the pressure, without increasing the frequency.

Marty must be willing to allow Lisa to choose when they will have sex and to set the pacing. Having the right to choose the time gives Lisa some of the control she needs to feel that her participation is voluntary. The agreement provides assurance for Marty that sex will occur, so he does not have to get so frantic about it and run over her for it. Naturally, he finds it difficult to trust her to do anything that he does not push. But even the most stubborn and mistrustful of us might be willing to commit to a trial agreement of two weeks or so, to see how it will work out. The obligation is limited and there is no major risk. But there are some real possibilities for benefit.

Trust is tenuous in these agreements, especially in the beginning. The entire arrangement is jeopardized the first time one or the other partner fails to comply with the letter of the agreement. When circumstances prevent them from getting together on schedule, Marty is quick to feel that the promise is false and that Lisa has betrayed the agreement. Another time, when he is interested and he asks if tonight is going to be one of the nights, Lisa is quick to read that as pressure and takes offense. Both must set their suspicions aside and allow the other some breathing room.

A contract to schedule sex is a remedy for a specific problem, not a permanent program for joyful sexual relationships. It might be compared to a cast for a broken arm, which is clumsy but serves the necessary function of holding the bone in place while the injury mends. Once sexual relations improve and trust is reestablished, the partners can introduce more freedom. Marty is eventually able to initiate sex some of the time, and have Lisa welcome his invitation. And Lisa gains the prerogative to say no in a way that is supportive rather than derogatory. Much rides on the way it is phrased. She tells him that she wants to make love to him later and suggests a time: "I'm worn out tonight, but I do want you. Can we get together tomorrow? Promise?" While she does not have to perform every time he asks, she nonetheless gives him the security that she does want him sexually.

It is sometimes surprising how pleased both partners can be with modest compromises. Twice a week would hardly seem to satisfy a fellow who seems to want it once or twice a night. But it does happen under the right conditions. One man who seemed absolutely insatiable said that good sex aroused him, but having it several times in two days would satisfy him for a week. He assured his wife that twice in one day would not add up to fourteen times a week, and she was willing to try clustering their times together. And true to his promise, several lovemaking sessions did indeed leave him satisfied and temporarily satiated. Between such binges, he was comfortable for several days at a stretch.

The quality of the sexual relationship is surely as important as the frequency, and compatibility is more a matter of complementary attitudes than of perfectly balanced drives. We look next at how several all-important relationship factors contribute to sexual satisfaction or dissatisfaction.

10

Conditions

Apparent imbalances in sexual interest may result from competing preferences not so much in the level of sexual activity but from requirements in how sexual relations proceed. The ideal situations captivate and arouse us, inviting treasured intimacy and warm passions, while unsatisfactory situations offend or frighten us or leave us merely unmoved and unfulfilled. Yearnings and fantasies combine with acceptable minimums to set the conditions for satisfactory sexual relationships.

The wife who appears uninterested in sex may simply be unsatisfied with how sex typically unfolds between her and her husband. Perhaps she wants him to go more slowly, or to talk to her more and be personally intimate before trying to be sexually intimate. Her real objection is not to sex itself but to the lack of romance and closeness that make the experience good for her. But her husband, who is pushing for more and better sex, fails to adjust to provide that closeness. Each partner wants sex on his or her own terms.

Competing Conditions

Women tend to want closeness and communication as a precondition for sex, while men usually prefer to proceed more quickly to intercourse. Women typically see sex as an expression of an already-existing relationship, while men want to use sex to establish warmth and intimacy in a relationship.[1] And while women want reassurance that men want them for more than just good sex, men look to good sex for reassurance that a woman really wants them.

Women—especially younger women—tend to value the tenderness before sex sometimes more than the intercourse itself.[2] Communication and foreplay set the mood, and without sufficient preparation, their arousal may be weak or absent. Women also are more likely to seek closeness immediately after sex as a way of unwinding from the excitement and affirming the connection. But to younger men, who are quickly aroused, the requirement for lengthy foreplay can be an unwelcome interruption and a jarring break in the natural progression. Young men tend to prefer women who are easily and quickly aroused—whose pacing more nearly matches their own.

But men and women do find ways to bridge these differences.

Courtship Bargains. One common tradition before marriage is called "courtship bargain" or "courtship barter," and takes the form of a competitive game.[3] The objective for males in the courtship barter is to move a relationship toward sexual intimacy, while the objective for females is to move the relationship toward closer emotional involvement and commitment. To make sex acceptable to her, the male must convince his partner that he finds her interesting and special, while to keep his interest, she must convince him that it is all going to be worth his while. Sex is in this sense a commodity. The boy who wants sexual favors is expected to court and romance the girl, while the girl who is romanced is expected to become more sexually intimate with him.

Although they appear competitive, these bargains provide something worthwhile to each of the participants. The successful trade-off produces a more complete relationship between the two, with the qualities of both commitment and sexual intimacy.

The tradition includes penalties for those who do not follow the rules. A fellow who makes no advances for the first few dates may be thought a gentleman, but if he makes no advances for six or ten weeks, the situation becomes awkward. His date wonders, "What's wrong with him?" Or, since we tend to take these things personally, "What's wrong with me?" Conversely, a woman who opens herself to sexual intimacies without requiring anything in return may cheapen the exchange so that the man wonders if she is too "easy."

Courtship barter is no longer required in today's freer and more versatile matching and mating. In a modern version, women have sex to explore the possibilities of a new relationship, then feel cheated if the commitment that was not there before sex does not appear after sex either. Many people have abandoned the barter routine altogether. Some women find a challenge in making sexual conquests and do not want a relationship, and some men want a commitment but are too insecure to be the sexual aggressor. Sexually freer women are regarded more favorably by a freer generation of men, who are less inclined to consider them "fallen" or "soiled." Many men are readily infatuated by women who are sexually eager for them, and they push for a commitment after intimacies. Nonetheless, some aspects of the traditional courtship bargain remain and frequently carry over into marriage. Impasses arise from failures to find agreeable trade-offs.

Impasses

Before marriage, the burdens of courtship often fall on the men, who make the invitations, pay for the tickets, and provide the music and the candles. Once married, new wives are often interested in continuing the romance, while their husbands may be uninterested in continuing to court them. Pamela, for example, became accustomed to special consideration leading to intimacies, and she does not want it to vanish now that she is married. Eddie, having taken on the responsibilities of marriage, does not feel that he should have to court and win his wife anew each time as if they were strangers. Whether they are dating or married, the romantic prelude carries a different meaning for women and men. To Pamela, romance means that she is truly cherished, while to Eddie, it indicates that he must earn his way into her heart.

Breakdowns in the trade-offs translate into some of the more typical complaints that men and women voice about each other. Pamela complains that Eddie is no longer a friend and companion to her and that intercourse without closeness is impersonal and unsatisfying. While an occasional quickie may be acceptable, she objects to fast intercourse every time, and afterward she feels cheated or used. Her issues are like those of single women, who complain that too many men rush the sexuality and are unwilling to take the time to get to know them. Eddie, in turn, complains that Pamela waits to be asked for sex but never initiates it, and that she responds too slowly and wants only the more personal face-to-face varieties of sex.

Why Not Compromise? Although preparation and foreplay tend to increase sexual responsiveness,[4] husbands often spend little time on these civilized amenities. Many men seem to not recognize the importance that women place on closeness and touch, as at least one survey suggests.[5] Men overestimate the importance to women of multiple orgasms, and they underestimate the importance of conversation and caresses before sex.[6] The misperceptions seem conveniently to resemble what men want to believe about women more than what women say about themselves. Men are more compelled by the passion of women's multiple orgasms than by the lead-in that precedes sex, and are using their own preferences in sex as a yardstick to measure those of their partners.

But it is more than a misperception. Men lean toward the faster pacing not just because it is more pleasurable but because a slower progression can feel awkward and uncomfortable to them, and unsafe as well. Eddie finds that the hugs and caresses that are so important to Pamela are often invitations to frustration and rejection for him, when she remains unwilling to follow them up with sex. Some men rush into sex out of fear that their arousal will not last, and that their equipment may fail by the time it is put to use.

Sex with little closeness leaves Pamela feeling used and unsatisfied, so that she requires still more consideration from Eddie before she can feel comfortable with him sexually.

How Much Is Enough? How much courtship and preparation do women require before they can respond wholeheartedly? Individual differences aside, the requirements vary according to how a woman feels about her partner. The more appealing a woman finds him, the more passionate she is and the less preparation she needs to respond to him. In their courtship, when Pamela was infatuated with Eddie, she seemed to arouse herself on her way to a romantic rendezvous by reminiscing, anticipating, and fantisizing.

Conversely, the less appealing a woman finds her mate, the more she requires from him to interest her in sex. Now when Pamela is annoyed, she seems to require hours of reassurance and conversation and some visible concessions. After a squabble, Eddie has to allow her time to calm down and warm up to him. The wife who is broadly unsatisfied with her husband may want not only more conversation, but also that he be more sensitive, more communicative, more compassionate, calmer, and livelier. She would be sexually interested only on the unlikely condition that he change into someone else.

Sex is an obvious area in which a woman can accept or reject a man as a sweetheart, and its significance in this respect continues into marriage. Eddie takes her sexual interest to mean that she loves and accepts him, and her sexual indifference feels like a loss of intimacy and an emerging chasm between them. He reads her requirement for conversation and touch not as a prelude to better sex but as indifference toward him and as sexual rejection.

Power Plays. Many men believe that their wives use sex as a bargaining chip to get what they want, or as a weapon when it is withdrawn to punish. Pamela's sexual indifference after a squabble serves to reinforce Eddie's belief that she is withdrawing sex as a punishment, to be reinstated only on the condition that he does what she wants him to do to make up with her. But to comply with her conditions seems to him too much like capitulation, signaling subservience, emasculation, weakness, and acquiescence to the feminine manner of lovemaking. Eddie wants Pamela to be attracted to him because of his inner qualities or his raw animal magnetism, not because he works for it by playing up to her. Unwilling to be manipulated, he refuses to concede. The price of the admission ticket is too high for him, and he tries to push his way in or to sneak in. Since her rejections are frequent, he works to protect himself by making himself insensitive to her opinions. Unwilling to pay the price of admission, he does without the small-time romance altogether and watches big-time football on his big-screen television instead.

Pamela too believes sex is being used for a power play—but by her husband. She feels that Eddie pushes her sexually to force her to give in to him and to have his way without considering her wishes. She is not about to give in and allow him to so control her, which would set a bad precedent.

Outcomes. Touch between men and women in this pattern becomes nearly impossible. When Pamela is physically affectionate at all, she arouses him sexually, and when Eddie becomes sexual rather than affectionate, he offends her. "Why can't you ever touch me without making it into something sexual?" she asks, injuring his pride and stirring his resentment. "Why don't you ever want sex?" he implores, suggesting the problem is that she is frigid or a prude. He is indifferent to her warmth when it does not lead to sex, and she is indifferent to sex that is not preceded by closeness.

Pamela wants Eddie to come to bed with her sometimes and hold her and be with her, allowing that it might lead to sex but with no guarantee. Eddie feels too frustrated by her and would require the guarantee. So they fall into a routine of separate bedtimes, each feeling rejected and blaming the other.

The woman in this pattern wants to be companions and not just sex partners with her husband, while the man wants to be lovers and not just good friends. She would love to be more passionate with him if he spent more time with her, and he would love to be more involved if she were sexually interested. But these conditions are implicit. She argues for more affection and against sex, not for one followed by the other. Annoyed by his insensitivity, she is unwilling to sweeten her invitation with a promise that the hugs will turn into sex. For his part, he is too annoyed to take the chance and give her what she wants. The conditions remain unsatisfied, and the pattern perpetuates itself (figure 10–1).

Age Changes the Conditions. As sexual interests change with age, the traditional arrangements lose their hold. By middle age, men are in better control of their less pressing sexual impulses. This has its up side and its down side, for middle-aged men find it easier to slow their pacing but are less interested in courting. The tables may turn so that the husband becomes the one who is unavailable for sex after an argument or when he feels annoyed or mistrustful, while the wife yearns for more involvement, including

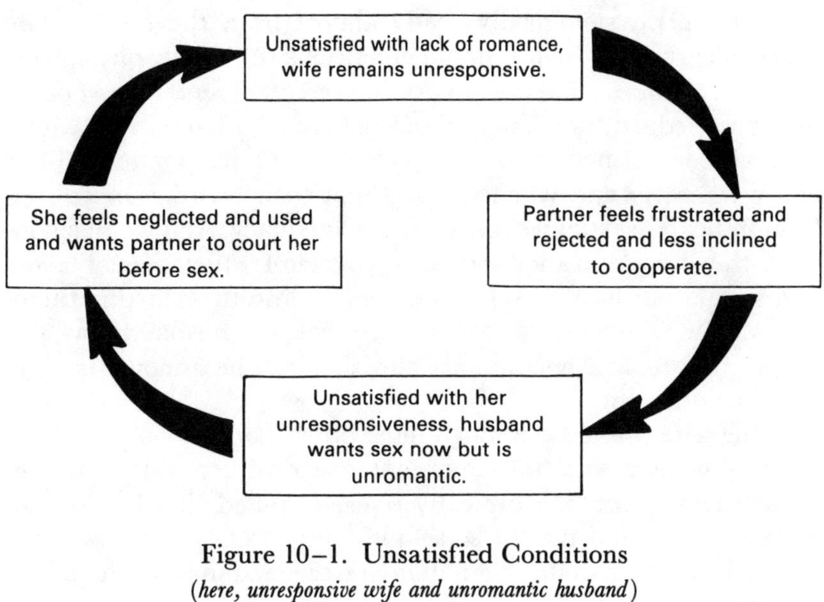

Figure 10–1. Unsatisfied Conditions
(*here, unresponsive wife and unromantic husband*)

sexual involvement, as a way of making up and maintaining the connection.

By middle age, many men are simply unable to respond sexually to women whom they perceive as cold, critical, or bitchy. Now it is the man who feels too vulnerable to participate in an intimate act with a partner who seems to care not about his feelings but only about herself. The man who is less interested in sex can also withhold it so that it is his wife who must make up before sex, or do without. Such arrangements run against the traditional expectations, but they are commonplace nonetheless among married couples.

For both genders, physiological responsiveness also changes. Arousal for men becomes slower and more tenuous, while it becomes quicker for women. By their fifties, many men require manual stimulation to achieve an erection,[7] while for many women in their thirties and after childbearing, vaginal lubrication—indicating physiological readiness—occurs almost instantly.[8] So older men must rely on their partners to slow the pacing and provide the physical stimulation to prepare them for sex, while middle-aged women are physiologically ready almost from the outset. The years thus reverse the minimum conditions set by our physiology.

Such changes seem uncomfortable and often remain unspoken, unacknowledged, and unaccepted between husbands and wives. At a basic level, men continue to believe that a real man should be ready wherever and whenever and that their own failure to perform indicates sexual weakness and inadequacy. And women continue to believe that they should be courted for their sexual favors and should not have to take charge of and do the courting themselves. The wife who wants sex more than her husband may still expect him to win her interest and she may be annoyed at him when he does not.

One wife wanted sex much more often than her husband, but she also wanted him to be more interested in her. When he suggested having sex, she typically refused, miffed that he was not more involved and that he so seldom initiated anything. Not surprisingly, he lost whatever small interest he had in her, which hurt her more. Used to contending with men as sexual aggressors, she did not understand that it was now her turn to court him. Perhaps we all identify too strongly with the familiar formative patterns of our youth and assume that they should continue, even when simple observation indicates they do not.

Better Bargains

Men and women might benefit simply by trying to understand each other more. The man who realizes that for his wife sex is an expression of their relationship will be more likely to hear her *no* as a request for closeness rather than as an attempt to manipulate him. And the woman who realizes that for her husband sex establishes closeness will be more likely to interpret his request for sex as an attempt to establish closeness. During a counseling session, Eddie tells Pamela that he has never felt so close and so in love with her as after they would make love earlier in their marriage, when she wanted him physically. Pamela had never fully realized that sex established such deep intimacy for him.

Only a few of the conditions partners typically set are bedrock requirements; most are only preferences, suggesting that there is room for negotiation and compromise. Women can adjust to briefer preliminaries and fantasize to get themselves in the mood, while men can adjust to lengthier preliminaries and even learn to like them.

Who Should Change? Customs in what men and women are supposed to find acceptable and satisfying in sex vary from culture to culture and even from decade to decade in the same culture. Perspectives in sex and marriage manuals change over the years, reflecting changes in the views of those who write them and of those who purchase them and seek their advice. A review of some forty-nine American sex manuals written between 1950 and 1980 identified quite separate philosophies over the decades.[9] The predominant philosophy of the sex manuals of the 1950s and 1960s was that women are not simply slower to become aroused than men but are naturally passive, requiring guidance and manipulation from their competent male partners. Cast as leader and teacher, the husband was seen as entirely responsible for the sexual experience. He was advised to be more patient in his pacing and more artful in his techniques for arousing his wife. The philosophy of manuals from 1975 to the present, by contrast, is that women are self-sufficient and independent agents, perfectly capable of managing their own responsiveness and responsible for their own satisfaction. The woman is advised to learn better ways to arouse and satisfy herself, with or without a man, quite on her own.

The manuals from the earlier era ask husbands to better meet the conditions their wives set, while those from more recent years suggest that wives forgo setting their usual conditions and learn to take the initiative themselves. Today's men may take heart that what is asked of them now is not so much compared with the earlier era, when sex was *all* their responsibility. Today's women, in turn, may realize that they can control much of their own experience rather than expect their husbands to do it for them.

Fight Elsewhere. Traditional wisdom advises us to avoid carrying outside squabbles into the bedroom, suggesting that sex be maintained as a sanctuary free and clear of everything else that goes wrong in a marriage. But obviously, a sexual relationship is not so readily separated from the rest of the relationship. Still, the principle is generally right and worth a try. The wife who demands that she get her way outside the bedroom as a precondition for sexual relations is courting a permanent chill in her marriage. Chances are, her husband gives in only begrudgingly or not at all, then pays her back in sullenness for what he sees as an unfair manipulation. She would do better to separate the fights and the sex, for giving her full attention to one or the other at a time would improve them both.

Partners who turn naturally to lovemaking after a fight say that the lovemaking is an unusually intimate experience, intensified by the excitement of having locked horns beforehand. Lovemaking after an argument confirms for both the stability of the relationship and an intimate connection that is not harmed by everyday and expectable clashes of wills. To some, it heals injuries left over from the fight and even of those from previous fights. One recently remarried man reported that he was surprised one day when his new wife wanted to make love to him after a particularly hot argument; not only was she willing, she seemed to want to be with him. He was surprised again the next day, when she continued the argument just as adamantly as before. He usually had slept on the couch after arguments with his first wife and had managed to adjust to it. He found that he was more comfortable in arguments with his present wife, more apt to state what he really felt rather than hold it inside and resent her for it. And he was more willing to listen to her and to compromise. Feeling secure that she loved him, he could admire her independence rather than feel threatened by it, and he considered her high-spirited and full of life. She too was comfortable arguing for what she wanted, assured that she could push her case without jeopardizing the security of the marriage.

Connecting Romance and Passion. Perhaps the most promising approach to fulfilling competing conditions is to link the romance that the one wants and the passion the other wants, so that they blend together in a unified experience suitable to both. The woman who wants more closeness before sex would do well to make the preludes safer and more pleasant for her partner. Suppose the husband tenders a sexual proposal for right now immediately, to which the wife is not agreeable at that moment but which she might want to take advantage of later on. If she responds with the bare-bones "I'm not in the mood," she squelches his interest. "You only get close to me when you want sex" is surely no improvement. "Why don't we just spend some time together, and we will see what happens?" is more neutral but still plays on his insecurities by suggesting that she does not really want him.

The wife who wants more intimacy beforehand might construct a firm connection between the closeness she wants and sexual passion. "Let's talk and get really close, then make love," she might suggest, connecting the two. "It would be nice to make love, but I want to be really close first" is another warm invitation. Such comments maintain the conditions she prefers, while the promise of sexual intimacy checks his frustration and provides appeal. She might openly state the implicit link between the preparation she wants and the passion he wants. "I want us to spend some time together and talk and hold each other so that I will be really aroused when we make love." How could he refuse?

Many men learn to appreciate the preparation when they are introduced to it properly. The attentiveness and closeness a wife may require can feel more like a comfortable beginning to the man rather than an unpromising obligation. He may begin to feel sensuous during the communication and caresses, secure that they will lead to sex but no longer in such a hurry. The trick is for her to ask for what she wants in a way that invites him to want it just as much as she does.

Why Me? A wife who wants to have closeness now and to wait to see how she feels about having sex later on might look more closely at the balance of power in her marriage. If she can keep her option of withholding sex afterward, he can keep his option of not involving himself beforehand.

Some women object to having to propose this or any other structure to a relationship on the grounds that the man should be more thoughtful and considerate on his own and should take charge and manage some of the romance himself. When you have to tell him how, it spoils the charm—or so it seems. Here again is the familiar problem of "expecting" someone to do something that he is not inclined to do, which results in annoyance with the person when he fails to meet your expectations. You would prefer that he do what you want on his own because he knows how to please you. But we live in an imperfect world that turns on its own principles, not on our personal fantasies. Your practical choices are to coach your husband to become more romantic, to stew over his failures, to give up on romantic fantasies altogether, or to look to fulfill them elsewhere. Given these choices, coaching an unromantic husband may not be the worst of all possible worlds after all.

Required Commitments. Similar solutions may work for unmarrieds as for marrieds. A woman may want to go slower and form a relationship first, while a man may want sex first as a condition for possibly beginning a relationship. Her simple "no" or "I'm not ready for sex" may suffice to put him off, but it can also ruffle feathers and create a rift that spoils any future possibilities. With a man who is really pushy, it might be just as well for her to shut the door. A woman who wants to leave the door open might ease the rejection by packaging her *no* with a promise of something better to come. "We would make much better lovers if we take some time and get to know each other first," she might suggest. Or, "I think that sex is best when you are best friends as well. Don't you agree?" She can even challenge him, as long as she frames it right: "If you're the sort of man who can manage a real relationship, we might have some fun together." The woman who believes that sex is wonderful in marriage and belongs there should say so. The man who is interested in a permanent relationship might accept the rain check, while the one who is not will not come back anyway.

Pleasant Preparations. Men too can look for better tie-ins between closeness and sex, benefiting themselves as well as their partners. You need not view the time before intercourse as a mere preparation for the real thing, to be tolerated because that is how you get what you really want. Rather, the preliminaries can and should provide some of the pleasantness of the experience they introduce, for men as well as for women. The objective is not to become a more considerate lover by learning to delay gratification—it's better to find gratification in the delay, recognizing that lengthening the sexual experience can also make it more satisfying. And a pacing that is more satisfying to the woman yields a vicarious satisfaction for the man, since most men find pleasure in women's pleasure.

Most women want to know that even when passion takes a night off, the warmth and love stay on. A man who stays close to his wife even when sex is off is saying to her that closeness matters to him too, and it can help her feel more comfortable about sexual intimacies in the nights that follow. So a compromise here is an investment in the future. A solid sense of security comes not from scoring every time but from knowing that your mate is really pleased with the lovemaking.

Men who are troubled by closeness that arouses them but then is not satisfied should talk to their partners about their feelings of frustration. Sometimes just labeling the feelings can be helpful; more communication, after all, is what women say they want most from men. Is it simple frustration, or is it more than that? Is it a sense of rejection, of withdrawal of affection, of abandonment? Does it include feelings of isolation from her and therefore loneliness or incompleteness in ways that cannot be quite specified? Putting the feelings into words can make them more understandable and more legitimate. Such feelings too often go unrecognized and unexplained, not because they are unusual or abnormal but because they seem awkward, impolite, immature, or selfish. So they go underground, only to surface later in anger or indifference toward a once-cherished sweetheart.

Women who want men to talk more about their feelings do not necessarily want men to have these sorts of feelings, real though they may be. But expressed with some sensitivity, they can be understood. Obviously, you will get farther expressing your feelings if you are not doing so to pressure someone into something. It's better to introduce such feelings when you are appreciating each other than in the midst of an angry quarrel over when and how often you have sex. While the feelings may seem awkward, they have a side that is quite legitimate. How is a fellow supposed to feel when they are home from a close and romantic evening together—and she finishes it off with an hour-long phone call to his mother-in-law in another time zone?

A man might think about what would make it more comfortable or pleasant for him to be closer and recognize that he has a right to state it. Once the conditions are specified, partners can work together to meet them.

It's Well Worth Your While. After being married a few years, it's natural for us to long for the steamy attraction of the first years together, when the chemistry or pure animal magnetism made great sex so easy that we almost took it for granted. It is surely normal to wish that it could continue that way, now and forevermore. Unfortunately, it's too easy to be miffed when it does not and to let the challenges of a maturing relationship go unmet. But we must all realize that the romantic rush of a new relationship is a temporary blessing, not an invitation to easy street or a free ride for the rest of our lives. Search we must for ways to understand each other and to find joy in the give-and-take that sustains a sexual relationship over the many years of a lasting marriage.

As a husband provides more closeness, his wife can be more sexually responsive; and as she provides more sexual security, he can be more comfortable with closeness. A positive pattern is established that takes on its own momentum.

11

Appreciation

Sex within marriage is special and sacred, it is argued, providing lasting pleasure while sweetening love and tightening the bonds between husband and wife. Surely the wonderful sensations should combine with the compliment of being wanted to produce a deeply affirming experience. Sharing intimate pleasures can make a good relationship richer and two separate individuals more complete.

Sex is necessarily a mutual experience, in which you look not just to your own sensations but to those of your partner too. You want to share the high rather than go it alone, and you want assurance that you are providing pleasure as well as partaking of it. Nobody wants to party by oneself in what is supposed to be a party for two. So in this peculiar activity, lovers look to each other for confirmation of their sexual acts and, more broadly, of their sexual identities.

But as we all know too well, many marriage partners find little to appreciate in their shared sexual relations, considering them awkward, too ordinary, too routine, and not beautifully satisfying in the ways sex is "supposed" to be. Somewhere along the way, the rush subsides, at least for a while, leaving one partner missing the magic and unsatisfied with what remains. And when one partner considers sex unsatisfactory, the chances are good that the other partner will soon find it unsatisfactory as well. The lack of appreciation has immediate consequences for the quality of the sexual relations, in a pattern characterized not so much by what the partners do but by what is missing.

Is Good Performance the Spice? Some people blame childhood inhibitions for their unsatisfactory sex lives, while others blame inhibited partners. Most blame the simple and ordinary routineness of marital sex. Today's marriage manuals advise that we become more adept at sex, improve our competencies, and venture out into new and more stimulating variations. Conservatives counter that sex has been oversold, so that expectations are now too high and everyone is too quickly disappointed by what should be accepted as average satisfactory sex. Obviously, no relationship can live up to the mythical standard of intensely pleasurable multiple orgasms (hers), brought about by a masterful and properly paced performance (his), culminating in a grand finale (simultaneously), followed by blissful calm and a spiritual rejuvenation that leads naturally into a repeat of the whole wonderful sequence.

But the problem is surely more than runaway expectations. Individuals have found ways to turn sex into a failure experience over many generations, long before the "joy of sex—more is better—anything goes" philosophy. Variety can be interesting or at least not harmful, although the continuing search for new experiences can itself become a routine. Perhaps we can be open to variations and yet continue to appreciate the more standard and ordinary experiences. Our focus should be on the love and sharing in a marriage, which may or may not be improved upon by additional variety.

Half Full or Half Empty? At the heart of the matter are the competing tendencies that we all have to cherish what is good in our sexual relationship and to stew about what is lacking. In sex, as in any experience, we always have the option either to focus on what we do have and be grateful, or to compare it with something better that we don't have and feel cheated. Does a man find her gentleness to be pleasing, or does the lack of heavy breathing mean that she has no vitality or passion? Is a woman pleased that he wants her so much, or does the pressure to oblige him turn sex into just another duty? Do you wish that you could really have someone from your fantasies, or are you thankful that you have someone for real? Is your cup half full, however these cups are measured, or half empty?

Those who focus on what is missing do so for what may seem to be good reasons. Imbalanced sexual interest may cause both partners to focus on how sex is unsatisfactory, as one pushes for more while the other wants to douse the passion. Some complain about sex to support an argument for more intimacy beforehand.

Even people who are reasonably satisfied with their sex life may find it awkward to seem too appreciative. Many couples say little to each other that is truly personal about any aspect of their relationship, so the absence of shared intimacies and compliments in the sexual realm is therefore not surprising. But by some mix of our deepest yearnings and our most obvious insecurities, this is where many of us want to be most warmly understood. Our reluctance to voice feelings here may be not just shyness but the manifestation of broader concerns in the give-and-take of sexual intimacies.

Who Ought to Be Grateful?

The specialness of sexual relations is an offering or gift to be given and received. In what is taken as the normal and ideal situation, both partners want sex at the same hour and with similar intensity, and both please and are in turn pleased in about the same amounts so that the giving and the receiving are truly mutual and balance out evenly. In practice, it does not ordinarily happen that way. In any given instance, one partner usually wants sex more and initiates it, and one partner is usually considered to be gaining more sexual pleasure and satisfaction from the act. In many relationships, in spite of the ideal, sex is often seen and treated as a favor, provided by one to be enjoyed by the other.

Sex may be sometimes more pleasuring for the man, sometimes for the woman, depending on who is more in the mood for it at the time. Alternating between being the pleaser and being pleased adds interesting variety and balances out nicely between partners. You can gain pleasure yourself, then turn the tables later; it is more enjoyable to give your mate pleasure when you know you are getting your share too.

Fairness matters. Are you getting as good as you are giving, or is someone taking advantage of your good nature? As in any trade, the value of the goods and services must be negotiated, and in sex this is especially true. How much is the pleasure and fulfillment worth? How much satisfaction are you finding in sex, and how much are you providing your mate? We do not tally these things on paper, which would be cold-hearted, and when the trade-off is fair enough, we seem not to notice it at all. But when someone figures he or she is getting shorted, watch out!

While pundits of the "me generation" suggest that the real action is in our own sensations, from stimulation through orgasm, much of the fulfillment of lovemaking comes through the eyes of our beloved. Most of us find it infinitely more flattering to be wanted than to long for an indifferent partner, and more honorable to please our beloved than to care only about our own pleasure. Following are some typical attitudes men and women have about pleasing and being pleased.

What Men Want Women to Want. Perhaps men's most frequent and most prominent sexual fantasy and preference is that the woman be truly involved in the experience. What men want most is for the woman herself to be interested and aroused, active in the lovemaking and pleased by it. In a broad survey of some four thousand men, passion in the woman was seen as the most important factor in men's sexual satisfaction.[1] The majority of the men—60 percent—said that they were most irritated by women who seem cold or uninterested while having sex, while only a few—a mere 5 percent—said they were put off by women who make the first advance, who make demands, or who seem "too easy." Asked what their partners could do to make sex more exciting, the most frequent suggestion—from 34 percent of the men—was, "Be more active!"

Active participation is stimulating, but the appeal involves more than simply the additional noise and thrashing about. The actively involved woman seems to be doing something to satisfy herself rather than just accommodating the man, which matters a great deal. As long as she is really interested, the two are full partners in a joint adventure. Passionless compliance suggests that the experience is just to console or to placate, and many men object to the suggestion that a sexual favor has been granted and that they are afterward obligated. The familiar "I am not at all interested, but if you insist . . ." may be imagined to include an unspoken corollary: ". . . then you are conducting this unseemly and inconvenient act upon me, and you owe me for it." Nobody wants to feel so beholden.

Today, amid the concern about male sexual insecurities, it is interesting that so many men claim they accept sexually demanding women and are put off by women who ask for nothing for themselves. The common performance anxieties about premature ejaculation or impotence are not about missing some pleasure but are rooted in men's intense fears about failing to provide pleasure for a woman. So the woman who knows what she wants and goes after it tends to set men at ease, contrary to expectations, simply because she herself is more committed to her own pleasure.

Knowing that women love sex seems to provide men with a comforting answer to their various unspoken sexual confusions and insecurities. More than any other form of compliment, it is a woman's pleasure that many men read as genuine appreciation.

What Women Want. In the face of persistent pressure to go wild in sex or at least to appear to do so, many women wish for some leeway to slow up and find comfort in intimacy without always having to push for passion. Sexual gratifications may be classed broadly as "traditional" and "modern," on the basis of whether sex is treated as a favor meriting compensation or as a pleasure in itself. It can be both, and it often is, but the distinction matters. In the traditional perspective, a proper woman accepts sex to begin a family and to maintain a marriage, and doing it for lust or for money is considered improper.

Today in the industrialized world, most women seek their own pleasure in sex, or feel they ought to, so that sex, like virtue, is its own reward. Now it is not merely pleasant, it is normal and healthy for a woman to love sex, and it is considered backward of her not to. When women enjoy sex, they lower the pressure on their husbands, who are no longer the perpetrators of an unwanted activity, and the change is undoubtedly much for the better for all involved. An active partner is more pleasing and, gaining the best of both worlds, the woman who finds sexual pleasure is cherished and appreciated for it.

Yet the modern perspective retains an uneasy trade-off with the more traditional one. If women now love sex themselves, does that mean they are no longer entitled to any special consideration for providing sex for men? If sex is for her as much as for him, does he bear no obligation to her because she is his lover? Not every woman who finds pleasure in sex is willing to give up the entitlements that traditionally go with providing sexual favors. And in spite of our modern times, some women still feel that doing things for themselves rather than for the benefit of others is improper. Sex for oneself may seem uncomfortably selfish.

Standoffs. Such concerns about who is the real beneficiary in sexual relations date all the way back to some of the earliest Western literature. In one ancient Greek myth, Zeus and Hera, the king and queen of the gods, are quarreling, as Greek gods are apt to do, over whether the male or female gets more pleasure out of lovemaking. You can guess which position each of them argues. As their umpire, they choose Teiresias,[2] a young herdsman who by extraordinary circumstances had once been changed into a woman, thereby experiencing lovemaking as a woman for seven years, and then changed back into a man. Teiresias ruled that the greater pleasure was given to the woman:

> Of ten, the man enjoyeth but one part,
> Nine parts the woman fills, with joyful heart.[3]

Hera was infuriated by Teiresias' pronouncement, and she punished him by making him blind. But Zeus later compensated him by giving him the gift of prophecy and a long life.

We are not told the circumstances of the quarrel, but they are easy enough to imagine. Zeus wants to believe that his lovemaking is greatly satisfying to his wife (and to many women, he being a freewheeling philanderer), while Hera wants to control his raging ego and gain some credit for the many sacrifices she makes in being his wife. He boasts that women gain great pleasure in sex, and she counters that women are just doing it to please men.

Since Greek myths were told by men, the favorable ruling from Mount Olympus is not too surprising. A female authority could easily arrive at the opposite conclusion, as Joyce Brothers does, to support her suggestion that young women are used in living-together arrangements and should hold out for marriage: "If a woman is willing to move in with a man and provide . . . sex without expecting anything much except an orgasm in return, that is all she is going to get. And since most women only reach orgasm about half the time," she argues "there is no way she is going to get as much out of it as he does."[4] A sexologist could note that women also have multiple orgasms, which is not quite pertinent, since the real concern is not in the tally of orgasms. The point is that even a modern woman who enjoys sex, wanting a claim to marriage or a ploy in the intimate infighting, can still argue that she gets less pleasure from it than does her fellow. And since only she knows her own experience, the Greek gods now remaining silent, it is her option to call it as she wishes.

In the politics of intimate relations, it can seem risky for either partner to appear too appreciative. The wife who likes sex still wants to be credited for providing a pleasant favor to her husband and therefore may do little to suggest that she is genuinely pleased with the experience herself. The woman who feels she is expected to perform may simply refuse, so that her passivity becomes an assertion of independence. If a quarrel erupts in the bedroom, a careless wife may mention that she does not really enjoy sex as much as it might appear and hasn't for a long while (thereby inflicting mortal injury). Even a gentle observation that "sex is not as important to me as it is to you" is apt to offend, even if true, usually more than the woman realizes and surely much more than the fellow is inclined to let on. The husband in this pattern wants to be assured by heavy breathing and great passion in his wife. He counts her orgasms, but he gives no indication that he himself finds anything particularly special about their meetings.

When it is the husband who pushes for sex, his message is usually paradoxical: "I want you to do it because you love it, not because I want you to." In a sour mood his message is: "Do it, but it isn't that wonderful, so don't think you are doing me any great favor." Just such statements contribute to the impersonal "just getting our rocks off" atmosphere of some sexual relations. And when the positions are reversed and the wife wants sex more frequently, she feels awkward and unwanted and lets her husband know that she does not appreciate always being the one to ask. By now sex feels routine and unimaginatively boring for both. One partner who seems unappreciative makes the other less appreciative as well, so that the pattern perpetuates itself (figure 11–1).

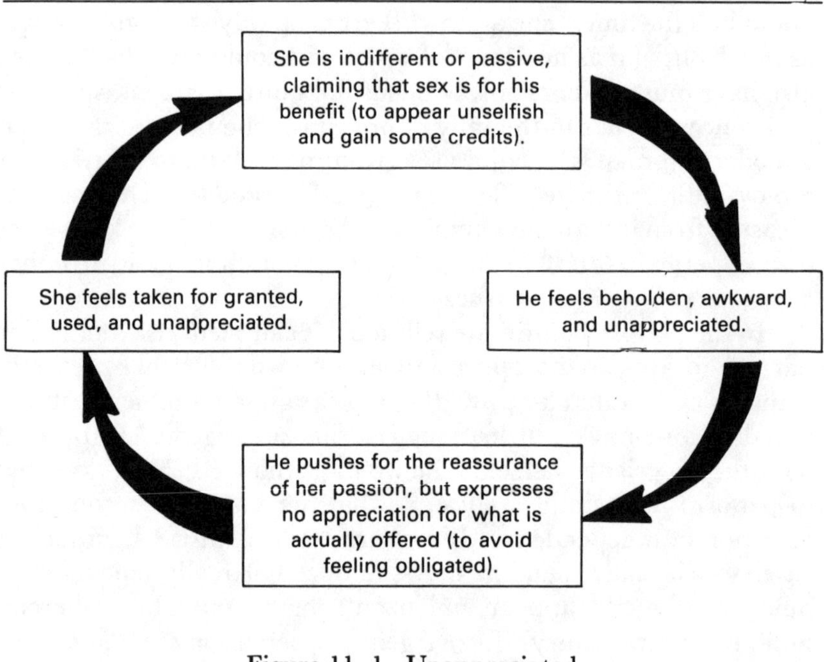
She is indifferent or passive, claiming that sex is for his benefit (to appear unselfish and gain some credits).
He feels beholden, awkward, and unappreciated.
He pushes for the reassurance of her passion, but expresses no appreciation for what is actually offered (to avoid feeling obligated).
She feels taken for granted, used, and unappreciated.

Figure 11–1. Unappreciated

Cherished Communication

How can we overcome sexual boredom? Although the usual prescription is to explore more and wider variations of activity, it is the reach and caress of communication that seems most vital. We need to say more about ourselves to each other to show up better as real people interested in sex. Couples find greater excitement when they rely on their own imaginations and share their fantasies, according to one study, than when they introduce erotic books or pictures to turn themselves on.[5] Talking together about feelings and fantasies invites a special and personal connection that is often otherwise missing between partners.

Some of the suggestions that follow were originally devised as ways to win back straying husbands, but they work even better in marriages that are beset by boredom but as yet uncomplicated by an extramarital affair. The suggestions for women are followed by suggestions for men. The focus here is not on improving sexual performance but on expressing appreciation for what may be already there.

Words Fascinate. Since men are normally pleased by women's interest in sex, talking about your immediate experiences stands out as the most obvious way to liven up a boring sexual relationship. You may not have to *do* more—only to be more outgoing about it.

Diane, the wife of the workaholic, began calling her husband at work and telling him she was fantasizing about him and that she just wanted to hear his voice. Her calls quickly started him fantasizing. What sort of fantasies was Diane having, he wondered, and what did she have in mind? What was she expecting him to do about them?

Plan something to say to your husband that fits for you. In the morning, you might tell your husband that you had a sexy dream about him, or that you always wake up warm and mellow after making love. Just a few such comments can go a long way. If nothing feels quite comfortable now, try something anyway, and you will probably become comfortable with it.

If you do not and cannot fantasize about your husband but want to, go ahead and say you are fantasizing. Then make up something and talk about the sort of fantasy that you wish you were having. As you tell about your pretend fantasy, you will get involved in it—and that is all you have to do to have a real fantasy. A fantasy is, after all, just something you make up.

This brings us to an important principle. Those who learn to talk about liking sex are more likely to find that they really *do* like it. Talking about your own pleasures can itself be interesting, and seeing how easily it interests your fellow makes it even more interesting.

Those who do not like to talk during sex can talk about it before or after, with similarly good results. A warm "I really loved that with you last night" may be all that is required. Maybe sex is like other performances, in that you must wait for the reviews the next morning to see how well you have done.

One couple had sexual relations in silence for some twenty years, by which time the husband was losing interest. He was quite surprised during one session when his wife said that she liked sex and really missed having it more frequently. Having never heard otherwise, he had been nurturing a mild grudge because he thought she was just doing it for him. The next few nights, he was much more interested. If she wants him to stay interested, she would do well to continue mentioning her own desire and not let him forget it.

The sixties "If it feels good, do it!" slogan is better advice for sex in marriage than for life in general. A modest variation may also fit nicely in your bedroom: "If it feels good, say it!" At least say it sometimes, and see if saying it feels good.

Talking about pleasures comes naturally for some women, while others must plan out what to say, then work up their confidence. Those women who find it easiest to attract men are often those who are quite forthright and open about their interests. When an ordinarily faithful husband is suddenly smitten with another woman, the chances are that she is talking to him about *her* sexual fantasies. Surely those racy conversations belong in a marriage more than outside a marriage.

Is Pleasure Selfish? Those who are concerned that seeking their own pleasure is too selfish should consider what they mean by being selfish. Properly, the word *selfish* means taking more than your share at somebody else's expense.[6] It is perhaps a paradox of altruistic sex that those who are most readily pleased themselves are usually most pleasing. Since your own pleasure is ordinarily pleasing to your husband, it cannot be selfish. See it as generous and considerate, then enjoy being generous and considerate. Those who consider it selfish to do anything at all pleasing for themselves tend to be miserable and to make those around them miserable as well. It *is* selfish to be blatantly inconsiderate of your partner, or to use sex manipulatively, to take unfair advantage, or to punish. Other than that, all is fair in the warmth of lovemaking.

Some women have husbands who seem to require an orgasm of them every time. Some women simply fake it, but many find this objectionable. Aside from this, consider the underlying question. Such a man fears that his wife does not really care about sex or about him, and he is looking for her orgasm as proof that she does. Other forms of proof may count just as well. Talk about what gives you pleasure in sex besides orgasm. Do you like the way he holds you, or the way his skin feels against your skin? Do you rest better afterward? Say so, and see if it reassures him. (If you do fake it, you do not need to correct the record later on, in the midst of an argument. Leave it faked.)

Fight Fair. Your proclamations that you love sex do not require you to give in on your other prerogatives. Claire worked as a legal secretary, then came home to manage the children and the housework, while her husband taught a few guitar lessons and played odd gigs around town. She appreciated his joy in living and his patience with their children, but she wanted him to take on his share of the workload. At bedtime, when he wanted sex and she was worn out, she steadfastly refused. He accused her of not wanting sex, but she never let him get away with that one. She argued back that she liked sex—she liked it a lot—but that she was plain-and-simple too tired for it. Or she said that she liked sex but was too mad at him to do it. He complained that he missed having a sex life, and she countered that she missed it just as much as he did. She insisted that he do his share of the workload and set that as a basic condition for sex. Once, appearing warm and flirtatious, she said she liked sex, but she was not sure she liked him. So they sparred, week after week. She held out for what she wanted, but in a manner that proclaimed her sensuality and that continued to fascinate him. Over several months, charmed by her in spite of himself, he took on a fairer share of their responsibilities.

The single woman who wants to hold out for marriage or at least a committed relationship need not argue that she enjoys sex less than her partner to avoid being pushed into it before she is ready. She can just as easily argue that she enjoys it too much and finds it too pleasurable and therefore does not want to be so vulnerable with someone she cannot count on. Appreciating sex need not mean being easy.

What Women Count as Appreciation. Most women do not interpret being wanted sexually to mean being loved, as men tend to do. Many women simply expect men to be readily aroused, based on their early experiences, and so they take it for granted (until later on, when arousal is no longer spontaneous). Since men seem to go off automatically, it makes little sense for women to count their partner's orgasms.

Again, further communication is important. Since simple sexual interest does not carry the message on its own, women want to hear men *say* what sex means to them. Sending flowers the morning after, or chocolates or balloons, are conventional ways to say that someone is special. You can give the same compliment by mentioning what you appreciate about your sexual experience. Tell her what it means to you. A truly personal comment matters more to most wives than most men think it possibly might or rightfully should mean.

Men who push for sex might ask themselves how and how often they show their wife that they really appreciate it. Aside from simply wanting sex and going after it, what do you do that says you cherish the meeting? While it is easy for men to joke about sex, they seem to find it awkward to say much about their actual experiences. Perhaps surprisingly, women seem more comfortable doing so than men. Sex therapist Ruth Westheimer observes that many women speak shamelessly about intimate experiences, "as though talking about cookie recipes at a church social."[7] Seldom do the husbands I talk with seem comfortable describing what they do in the bedroom with their wives.

But it is important for men to talk about their experiences, in spite of the awkwardness. Ask yourself the obvious questions: What do you like about sex with your wife? Do you like how she holds you during lovemaking? Do you like what she says, what she does, how she smells? What do you most like about how she looks? Tell her!

Sometimes the most important things are vague and hard to formulate. Perhaps sex with your wife makes you feel calmer, more comfortable with yourself, better connected. Does the fact that she gives herself to you make you feel that she really must love you? Does she seem warm and sensitive to you when you make love? Do you count on her wanting you more than you think is proper, and would you be lost and lonely without her lovemaking? Do real men say things like this? Take a few moments, and search for some of your most personal feelings about sex with her. And say a few words to her about them.

A few years into a marriage, when formerly insatiable appetites want a few nights off, it is important to understand what is happening. Sexual arousal usually diminishes for men when they are stressed or overworked, and when frequent sex becomes routine. When the wife is ready to go, it now falls on the husband to explain to her that lower libido does not mean less love. This is a good time to talk about the importance of the companionship, your sense of security, her cheerfulness, or whatever it is you cherish about your marriage.

Soak in the Assurances. Those who most require sexual reassurances can be those who are most set on not hearing them. Men who insist on orgasms every session would do well to broaden their specs for good lovemaking. Do your appreciate that your wife is open to you? Do you hear what she says she likes about being with you?

All of us could think more about appreciating what we are being offered. Accept it, cherish it, cultivate it. Meditate upon it, or pray if so inclined, in appreciation and gratefulness. More often than you might expect, it will flourish into something more beautiful.

As you become more forthright in saying what you love about sex, you make it easier for your partner to do the same. Be complimentary for a while, then ask your beloved to say something about what he or she likes about sex with you. Supportive conversations go a long way to reintroduce the assurance of love into lovemaking.

Perhaps you are not made for the truly heroic sex of the prime-time sexual athlete so honored in fantasies and sex manuals. Yet gentle lovers with warm hearts can and do learn to truly cherish each other, sometimes while doing much less than most of us now take for granted. Open yourself to the sweetness of your love, and soak it in until your half-empty vessels are reassuringly full.

Epilogue

People who are already wary of marriage may see the routines suggested in this book as evidence that they are better off uncommitted, continuing in serial relationships, or staying by themselves. And granted, some people are panicked by the thought of commitment or are too injured or too narcissistic to be suited for a long-term relationship. But most of us want the benefits of marriage and can adjust to it. We want to belong, and we want the security and the ongoing companionship. A whole string of temporary relationships cannot be tied together to form a single viable family.

While troublesome patterns do continue over years of marriage, unmarried relationships fare no better. Men and women are no more considerate of each other in romances than they are in marriages, and they are apt to be worse. Uncommitted relationships have just as many misunderstandings, just as many spats, and surely more heartbreaks than marriages. One study found that mate-battering among unmarrieds living together was four times as frequent as among marrieds.[1] Unmarrieds are thus more likely to find themselves in abusive situations, not less. The apparent freedom to come or go as you wish seems to provide no protection at all. Unmarrieds, who are freer to leave, are also less invested in the relationship and freer to mistreat each other while they are in it. Troublesome patterns may last longer in marriages, but this does not mean that they are more frequent or more severe.

Recognizing the possibilities for injury in intimate relationships, many counselors advise troubled individuals to stay away from serious involvements until they straighten out their lives and get their heads on straight. A familiar message of our ongoing "individuals first" culture is that individual growth should take precedence over a relationship, or at least precede it to prepare us properly for it. But we can grow in a marriage just as well.

"It is a mistake to assume that individual growth can take precedence over relationships," asserts Joel Block in his classic work on friendship. "We learn in friendship to look with the eyes of another person, to listen with another's ears and to feel with another's heart. . . . Friendship is training for living in a social world."[2] So too in marriage, where we learn to look with the eyes of another person or to pay for our blindness, and where we find ourselves in constant training for living in the most intimate of relationships.

Marriage offers important opportunities for growth that are seldom found outside a committed relationship. Problems that show up quickly in a marriage may be hard to identify at all before marriage. Hands-on experience seems to be a requirement. You must get into the water to learn to swim, and you must involve yourself in a relationship before you can work to improve it. Counselors who treat relationships usually try to see both members of any couple, at least occasionally, to see how they interact. Those who treat only individuals are likely to be flying blind, trusting in one-sided reports and in guesswork about what is happening in the homes where these individuals reside.

A committed relationship usually provides us with the time it takes to straighten out troublesome patterns. Unlike a new romance, where a poor first impression can be fatal, marriage gives us a second chance when we mess up, and maybe two hundred more chances and perhaps another two thousand chances after that. I am not saying to take it all for granted and lounge around and do nothing. But if you are genuinely interested in changing and want to search for joy together, the chances are that your marriage will allow you sufficient time for your journey. Remember that time is on your side.

Marriage also aligns you with a partner who may be quite interested in your welfare. Granted, in marriages at their worst, both partners seem to be out for numero uno and neither seems to care a whit about the other. But even in a stalemated marriage, when the partners sidestep their impasses and the hurt and bitterness, there is usually some concern. In most marriages, including those with their fair share of problems, the caring is warm and obvious. In any case, it is in the best interest of two individuals in the same boat to row together, if only because that is the only way either of them can get anywhere. Even committed adversaries let go of their feuds long enough to occasionally act in their own best interests.

Having seen many good people in terrible marriages and perhaps a few rotten people in seemingly good marriages, I would never want to say that most of us get what we deserve. But some of what we contribute over the years does have a way of coming back to us. Marriage tends to reward some of our traditional virtues. Planning pays off, and so do patience and persistence as we work for changes. Tolerance provides the necessary room to breathe, and a smattering of humility makes it easier for us to admit that we are wrong on those rare occasions when we are. The willingness to love is important, of course, especially when it includes honest concern and genuine compassion. You can love all that is beautiful and wonderful in your sweetheart, and you can also be in love with your romantic fantasies. But compassion is the willingness to see the failings and imperfections alongside the goodness, and to love anyway, perhaps all the more strongly because your love is needed.

Look for these good qualities in yourself, and try to grow into them. Take advantage of the opportunity at hand, and practice these inclinations in your most important relationship.

"You cannot count on anyone but yourself," we frequently are told in our individualistic society; and "Nobody can make you happy but yourself." These are good reminders for people who expect relationships to carry them along free of charge and who sulk and gripe and make themselves miserable when special treatment is not forthcoming. But most people in committed relationships can indeed count on each other, and most of us do look to our families for a reasonable share of our happiness. A good marriage can be emotionally healing, as love and trust soothe and gradually replace lingering injuries from earlier years. Growth need not be strictly an individual undertaking. You can become more right for one another, and you can grow together.

As is sometimes said, the truly healthy person is one who can make the same mistake twice and not get nervous about it.

Recognize that you must run through most of your patterns more than twice before you will resolve them, and then go easy on yourself as you do. It is also said that good psychological health does not mean being free of problems, but involves a string of new problems instead of the same old problems. So you need not worry that tossing your old patterns away will leave you with no stability in your life and nothing to do. You are sure to find a whole future of new challenges, along with new joys and perhaps richer fulfillment along the way.

May the spirit of your love together be with you always on your journey.

Notes

Chapter 1

1. As suggested by psychoanalytic writings, which propose unconscious conflict as the primary cause of maladjustment.
2. See R. Driscoll, "Self-Condemnation: A Comprehensive Framework for Assessment and Treatment," *Psychotherapy* 26 (1989): 104–11.
3. Ordinary language psychology involves the clarification and use of concepts from everyday language in lieu of concepts from theoretical frameworks. The ordinary language distinction between acts done on purpose and those that are accidents or mistakes or otherwise inadvertent is fundamental to understanding human behavior generally and troublesome actions in particular. Cf. R. Driscoll, "Ordinary Language as a Common Language for Psychotherapists," *Journal of Integrative and Eclectic Psychotherapy* 6 (1987): 485–94.
4. See J. Gottman, *Marital Interaction: Experimental Investigations* (New York: Academic Press, 1979).

Chapter 2

1. G. Rosen, "Self-Help Treatment Books and the Commercialization of Psychotherapy," *American Psychologist* 42 (1987): 46–51; R. E. Glasgow and G. M. Rosen, "Behavioral Bibliography: A Review of Self-Help Behavior Therapy Manuals," *Psychological Bulletin* 85 (1978): 1–23; and R. E. Glasgow and G. M. Rosen, "Self-Help Behavior Therapy Manuals: Recent Development and Clinical Usage," *Clinical Behavior Therapy Review* 1 (1982): 1–20.
2. These four stages have been attributed to Harold Mosak, a student of Alfred Adler.

Introduction to Part II

1. Standard estimates are that there are on the order of ten million cases of alcoholism in the United States, or approximately one in twenty adults.
2. It is estimated that half of husbands and a third or more of wives have at least one affair during the course of a marriage. See Frank Pittman, *Private Lies* (New York: W. W. Norton, 1989).

Chapter 3

1. Adapted from purposes of self-condemnation in R. Driscoll, "Their Own Worst Enemies," *Psychology Today* (July 1982): 45–49; and "Self-Condemnation: A Comprehensive Framework for Assessment and Treatment," *Psychotherapy* 26 (1989): 104–11.
2. I believe Groucho made this quip after being rejected by a club because he was Jewish.
3. This technique has been variously called reflexive listening (by Haim Genot), active listening (by Thomas Gordon), and empathic responding (when introduced by Carl Rogers).
4. Elaine Hatfield and G. William Walster, *A New Look at Love* (Lanham, Md.: University Press of America, 1978). See also A. Cohen and I. Silverman, "Repression-Sensitization as a Dimension of Personality" in B. A. Maher, ed., *Progress in Experimental Personality Research,* vol. 1 (New York: Academic Press, 1964).
5. Presented by Arlene Skolnick of the University of California at Berkeley and summarized in *Psychology Today* (December 1987): 6.

Chapter 4

1. This conclusion is from a survey of a thousand people in Michael McGill, *Changing Him, Changing Her* (New York: Simon and Schuster, 1982); cited in S. Naifen and G. Smith, *Why Can't Men Open Up?* (New York: Warner Books, 1985), 4–5.
2. The concept of "pursuers and distancers," along with some of their individual characteristics, was presented by Harriet Lerner in *The Dance of Anger* (New York: Perennial Library, 1985), 91.
3. In Lane Lasater, *Recovery from Compulsive Behavior* (Deerfield Beach, Fla.: Health Communications, 1988), 55.
4. Cited in Naifen and Smith, *Why Can't Men Open Up?*
5. Reported by Pamela Adelmann in *Psychology Today* (May 1989): 69.
6. Study reported on Public Radio, 1980.
7. In a survey of 83,000 women, reported by *Ladies Home Journal* (January 1983).
8. The difference between feeling love and meaning love was suggested by Peter Ossorio of the University of Colorado.

Chapter 5

1. E. Walster, G. W. Walster, and E. Bersheid, *Equity Theory and Research* (Boston: Allyn and Bacon, 1978).
2. Givers' and takers' tendencies are similar to the nurturance and succorance factors in mate selection. See R. Winch, *Mate Selection* (New York: Harper,

1958). Complementarity as a general principle is poorly supported by the mate selection research, although some complementary factors may be important. See J. R. Eshleman, *The Family,* 4th ed. (Boston: Allyn and Bacon, 1985), 316–18.

3. Some of these dynamics are nicely presented in Dianne Hales, "Are You Too Good a Wife?" *Woman's Day* (May 10, 1988): 54–61. See also the generosity and anger variations of acquiescence and outbursts in chapter 8 of this book.
4. Joseph Heller, *Catch-22* (New York: Simon and Schuster, 1961).
5. James Dobson, *Love Must Be Tough* (Waco, Tex.: Word Books, 1983).
6. M. Wallach and L. Wallach, *Psychology's Sanction for Selfishness* (San Francisco: W. H. Freeman, 1983).
7. Erik Erikson, *Childhood and Society,* 2d ed. (New York: W. W. Norton, 1963).

Introduction to Part III

1. The quotations from Jefferson and Twain are juxtaposed in Carol Tavris, *Anger: The Misunderstood Emotion* (New York: Simon and Schuster, 1982), 122.

Chapter 6

1. See H. Toch, "The Management of Hostile Aggression: Seneca as Applied Psychologist," *American Psychologist* 38 (1983): 1022–26.
2. James Averill, *Anger and Aggression* (New York: Springer-Verlag, 1982).
3. Peter Ossorio, *Clinical Topics* (Boulder, Colo.: Linguistic Research Institute, 1966).
4. See the review in Stanley Strong, "Social Psychological Approach to Psychotherapy Research," in S. Garfield and A. Bergin, *Handbook of Psychotherapy and Behavior Change,* 2d ed. (New York: John Wiley, 1978), 122–24.
5. Thomas Gordon, *Parent Effectiveness Training* (New York: Peter Wyden, 1970).
6. Harriet Lerner, *The Dance of Anger* (New York: Perennial Library, 1985).

Chapter 7

1. James Averill, "Studies on Anger and Aggression," *American Psychologist* 38 (1983) 1145–160.
2. See Ray Bergner, "Emotions: A Conceptual Formulation and Its Clinical Implications," in K. E. Davis and R. Bergner, *Advances in Descriptive Psychology,* vol. 3 (Greenwich, Conn.: JAI Press, 1983).
3. See Richard Stuart, *Helping Couples Change* (New York: Guilford Press, 1980).
4. Source of this story unknown.

Chapter 8

1. Such as Harriet Lerner: "In contrast [to men], women have been denied the forthright expression of even healthy and realistic anger" (in "The Taboos against Female Anger," *Menninger Perspective* [Winter 1977], 5-11), and "The direct expression of anger, especially at men, makes [women] unladylike, unfeminine, unmaternal, sexually unattractive. . . . Our language condemns angry women as 'shrews,' 'witches,' 'bitches,' 'hags,' 'nags,' and 'castrators' " (in *The Dance of Anger* [New York: Perennial Library, 1985]). And Celia Halas writes that anger "is an emotion that women express far less frequently than do men. In fact, men generally feel quite comfortable with anger, express it freely, and are reasonably careless about the problems it causes in other people. . . . Women are generally afraid to express their anger" (in *Why Can't a Woman Be More Like a Man?* [New York: Macmillan, 1981]). Reviewed in Carol Tavris, *Anger: The Misunderstood Emotion* (New York: Simon and Schuster, 1982), 122.
2. See John Nicholson, *Men and Women: How Different Are They?* (New York: Oxford University Press, 1984).
3. The conclusion here refers to modern Western culture.
4. D. Fitz, "Anger Expression of Women and Men in Five Natural Locations," paper presented to the American Psychological Association, New York, 1979. Summarized in Tavris, *Anger.*
5. James Averill, *Anger and Aggression* (New York: Springer-Verlag, 1982). See also W. Frost and J. Averill, "Sex Differences in the Everyday Experience of Anger," paper presented to the Eastern Psychological Association, Washington, D. C., 1978. Summarized in Tavris, *Anger.*
6. Sandra Thomas, principal investigator in health study, University of Tennessee (in progress).

Introduction to Part IV

1. Romantic and companionate love are compared in Elaine Hatfield and G. William Walster, *A New Look at Love* (Lanham, Md.: University Press of America, 1978); and in R. Driscoll, K. E. Davis, and M. Lipetz, "Parental Interference and Romantic Love: The Romeo and Juliet Effect," *Journal of Personality and Social Psychology* 24 (1972): 1–10.
2. T. Houston, S. McHale, and A. Crouter, "When the Honeymoon Is Over," in R. Gilmore and S. Duck, eds., *The Emerging Field of Personal Relationships* (Hillsdale, N.J.: Lawrence Erlbaum, 1986).

Chapter 9

1. B. Zilbergeld and P. Kilmann, "The Scope and Effectiveness of Sex Therapy," *Psychotherapy* 21 (1984): 319–26.

2. Helen Singer Kaplan, *Disorders of Sexual Desire* (New York: Simon and Schuster, 1979).
3. B. Zilbergeld and C. R. Ellison, "Desire Discrepancies and Arousal Problems in Sex Therapy," in S. Leiblum and L. Pervin, eds., *Principles and Practice of Sex Therapy* (New York: Guilford Press, 1980).
4. H. S. Kaplan and C. J. Sager, "Sexual Patterns at Different Ages," *Medical Aspects of Human Sexuality* (June 1971), 10–23.
5. See A. Kinsey, W. Pomeroy, C. Martin, and P. Gebhard, *Sexual Behavior in the Human Female* (Philadelphia: Saunders, 1953).
6. M. Hunt, *Sexual Behavior in the 1970s* (Chicago: Playboy Press, 1974).
7. Cited by J. Hyde, *Human Sexuality* (New York: McGraw-Hill, 1982), 342. *Redbook* survey, source unlisted.
8. Cited by R. Bell, *Premarital Sex in a Changing Society* (Englewood Cliffs, N.J.: Prentice-Hall, 1966), 137.

Chapter 10

1. R. Bergner and L. Bergner, "Sexual Misunderstandings: A Descriptive and Pragmatic Formulation," *Psychotherapy* (in press).
2. N. W. Denney, J. K. Field, and D. Quadagno, "Sex Differences in Sexual Needs and Desires," *Archives of Sexual Behavior* 13 (1984): 233-46; and A. Pietropinto and J. Simenauer, *Beyond the Male Myth* (New York: Times Books, 1977). Reviewed in Z. Luria, S. Friedman, and M. Rose, *Human Sexuality* (New York: John Wiley and Sons, 1987).
3. W. Waller, *The Family: A Dynamic Interpretation* (New York: Holt, Rinehart and Winston, 1951). Supported in a review by J. R. Eshleman, *The Family* (Boston: Allyn and Bacon, 1974), 326-27.
4. P. H. Gebhard, "Factors in Marital Orgasm," *Journal of Social Issues* 22 (1966): 88–95.
5. Survey of one hundred "friends and acquaintances" in *The Village Voice*, reviewed in Luria et al., *Human Sexuality*, 427–28.
6. Reported in J. N. Gagnon, ed. *Human Sexuality in Today's World* (Boston: Little, Brown, 1977). Reviewed in Luria et al., *Human Sexuality*, 428.
7. H. S. Kaplan and C. J. Sager, "Sexual Patterns at Different Ages," *Medical Aspects of Human Sexuality* (June 1971), 10–23.
8. Ibid.
9. M. S. Weinberg, R. Swensson, and S. Hammersmith, "Sexual Autonomy and the Status of Women: Models of Female Sexuality in U. S. Sex Manuals from 1950 to 1980," *Social Problems* 30 (February 1980): 312–24. Summarized by J. Eshleman, *The Family*, 4th ed. (Boston: Allyn and Bacon, 1985).

Chapter 11

1. A. Pietropinto and J. Simenauer, *Beyond the Male Myth* (New York: Times Books, 1977).

2. H. J. Rose, *Handbook of Greek Mythology* (New York: E. P. Dutton, 1959).
3. C. Kerényi, *The Heroes of the Greeks,* trans. H. J. Rose (New York: Grove Press, 1960), 100. Used by permission.
4. Joyce Brothers, *What Every Woman Ought to Know About Love and Marriage* (New York: Random House, 1984), 128.
5. R. Baron and D. Byrne, *Social Psychology: Understanding Human Interaction,* 2d ed. (Boston: Allyn, 1977), as cited in J. McCary and S. McCary, *McCary's Human Sexuality,* 4th ed. (Belmont, Calif.: Wadsworth, 1982), 205.
6. *Webster's Ninth New Collegiate Dictionary* defines *selfish* as "seeking or concentrating on one's own advantage, pleasure, or well-being without regard for others."
7. Ruth Westheimer, *Dr. Ruth's Guide for Married Lovers* (New York: Warner Books, 1986), 78.

Epilogue

1. Associated Press wire service, 1989.
2. Joel Block, *Friendship* (New York: Collier, 1989).

Bibliography

Averill, James. *Anger and Aggression.* New York: Springer-Verlag, 1982.

———. "Studies on Anger and Aggression." *American Psychologist* 38 (1983) 1145–60.

Baron, R., and D. Byrne. *Social Psychology: Understanding Human Interaction.* 2d ed. Boston: Allyn, 1977.

Bell, R. *Premarital Sex in a Changing Society.* Englewood Cliffs, N.J.: Prentice-Hall, 1966.

Bergner, Ray. "Emotions: A Conceptual Formulation and Its Clinical Implications." In K. E. Davis and R. Bergner, *Advances in Descriptive Psychology,* vol.3. Greenwich, Conn.: JAI Press, 1983.

Bergner, Ray, and Laurie Bergner. "Sexual Misunderstandings: A Descriptive and Pragmatic Formulation." *Psychotherapy* (in press).

Block, Joel. *Friendship.* New York: Collier, 1980.

Brothers, Joyce. *What Every Woman Ought to Know about Love and Marriage.* New York: Random House, 1984.

Cohen, A., and I. Silverman. "Repression-Sensitization as a Dimension of Personality." In B. A. Maher, ed., *Progress in Experimental Personality Research,* vol. 1. New York: Academic Press, 1964.

Denney, N. W., J. K. Field, and D. Quadagno. "Sex Differences in Sexual Needs and Desires." *Archives of Sexual Behavior* 13 (1984): 233–46.

Dobson, James. *Love Must Be Tough.* Waco, Tex.: Word Books, 1983.

Driscoll, R. "Their Own Worst Enemies." *Psychology Today,* July 1982, 45–49.

———. "Ordinary Language as a Common Language for Psychotherapists." *Journal of Integrative and Eclectic Psychotherapy* 6 (1987): 485–94.

———. "Self-Condemnation: A Comprehensive Framework for Assessment and Treatment." *Psychotherapy* 26 (1989): 104–11.

Driscoll, R., K. E. Davis, and M. Lipetz. "Parental Interference and Romantic Love: The Romeo and Juliet Effect." *Journal of Personality and Social Psychology* 24 (1972): 1–10.

Erikson, Erik. *Childhood and Society.* 2d ed. New York: W. W. Norton, 1963.

Eshleman, J. *The Family.* 4th ed. Boston: Allyn and Bacon, 1985.

Fitz, D. "Anger Expression of Women and Men in Five Natural Locations." Paper presented to the American Psychological Association, New York, 1979.

Frost, W., and J. Averill. "Sex Differences in the Everyday Experience of Anger." Paper presented to the Eastern Psychological Association, Washington, D. C., 1978.

Gagnon, J. H., ed. *Human Sexuality in Today's World.* Boston: Little, Brown, 1977.

Gebhard, P. H. "Factors in Marital Orgasm." *Journal of Social Issues* 22 (1966): 88–95.

Glasglow, R. E., and G. M. Rosen. "Behavioral Bibliotherapy: A Review of Self-Help Behavior Therapy Manuals." *Psychological Bulletin* 85 (1978): 1–23.

———. "Self-Help Behavior Therapy Manuals: Recent Development and Clinical Usage." *Clinical Behavior Therapy Review* 1 (1982): 1–20.

Gordon, Thomas. *Parent Effectiveness Training.* New York: Peter Wyden, 1970.

Gottman, J. *Marital Interaction: Experimental Investigations.* New York: Academic Press, 1979.

Halas, C. *Why Can't a Woman Be More Like a Man?* New York: Macmillan, 1981.

Hales, Dianne. "Are You Too Good a Wife?" *Woman's Day,* May 10, 1988, 54–61.

Hatfield, Elaine, and G. William Walster. *A New Look at Love.* Lanham, Md.: University Press of America, 1978.

Heller, Joseph. *Catch-22.* New York: Simon and Schuster, 1961.

Houston, T., S. McHale, and A. Crouter. "When the Honeymoon is Over." In R. Gilmore and S. Duck, eds., *The Emerging Field of Personal Relationships.* Hillsdale, N.J.: Lawrence Erlbaum, 1986.

Hunt, M. *Sexual Behavior in the 1970s.* Chicago: Playboy Press, 1974.

Hyde, J. *Human Sexuality.* New York: McGraw-Hill, 1982.

Jacob, T. "Family Interaction in Disturbed and Normal Families: A Methodological and Substantive Review." *Psychological Bulletin* 82 (1975): 33–65.

Kaplan, Helen Singer. *Disorders of Sexual Desire.* New York: Simon and Schuster, 1979.

Kaplan, H. S., and C. J. Sager. "Sexual Patterns at Different Ages." *Medical Aspects of Human Sexuality,* June 1971, 10–23.

Kerényi, C. *The Heroes of the Greeks.* Trans. H. J. Rose. New York: Grove Press, 1960, 100.

Kinsey, A., W. Pomeroy, C. Martin, and P. Gebhard. *Sexual Behavior in the Human Female.* Philadelphia: Saunders, 1953.

Lasater, Lane. *Recovery from Compulsive Behavior.* Deerfield Beach, Fla.: Health Communications, 1988.

Lasch, Christopher. *The Culture of Narcissism: American Life in an Age of Diminishing Expectations.* W. W. Norton, 1978.

Lerner, H. G. "The Taboos against Female Anger." *Menninger Perspective,* Winter 1977, 5–11.

———. *The Dance of Anger.* New York: Perennial Library, 1985.

Luria, Z., S. Friedman, and M. Rose. *Human Sexuality.* New York: John Wiley and Sons, 1987.

McCary, J., and S. McCary. *McCary's Human Sexuality.* 4th ed. Belmont, Calif.: Wadsworth, 1982.

McGill, Michael. *Changing Him, Changing Her*. New York: Simon and Schuster, 1982.

Naifen, S., and G. Smith. *Why Can't Men Open Up?* New York: Warner Books, 1985.

Nicholson, John. *Men and Women: How Different Are They?* New York: Oxford University Press, 1984.

Ossorio, Peter. *Clinical Topics*. Boulder, Colo.: Linguistic Research Institute, 1966.

Pietropinto, A., and J. Simenauer. *Beyond the Male Myth*. New York: Times Books, 1977.

Pittman, Frank. *Private Lies*. New York: W. W. Norton, 1989.

Rose, H. J. *Handbook of Greek Mythology*. New York: E. P. Dutton, 1959.

Rosen, G. "Self-Help Treatment Books and the Commercialization of Psychotherapy." *American Psychologist* 42 (1987): 46–51.

Strong, Stanley. "Social Psychological Approach to Psychotherapy Research." In S. Garfield and A. Bergin, *Handbook of Psychotherapy and Behavior Change*. 2d ed. New York: John Wiley, 1978, 122–24.

Stuart, Richard. *Helping Couples Change*. New York: Guilford Press, 1980.

Tavris, Carol. *Anger: The Misunderstood Emotion*. New York: Simon and Schuster, 1982, 122.

Toch, H. "The Management of Hostile Aggression: Seneca as Applied Psychologist." *American Psychologist* 38 (1983): 1022–26.

Wallach, M., and L. Wallach. *Psychology's Sanction for Selfishness*. San Francisco: W. H. Freeman, 1983.

Waller, W. *The Family: A Dynamic Interpretation*. New York: Holt, Rinehart and Winston, 1951.

Walster, E. "Equity and Extramarital Sexuality." *Archives of Sexual Behavior* 7 (1978), 121–41.

Walster, E., G. W. Walster, and E. Bersheid. *Equity Theory and Research*. Boston: Allyn and Bacon, 1978.

Weinberg, M. S., R. Swensson, and S. Hammersmith. "Sexual Autonomy and the Status of Women: Models of Female Sexuality in U. S. Sex Manuals from 1950 to 1980." *Social Problems* 30 (February 1980): 312–24.

Westheimer, Ruth. *Dr. Ruth's Guide for Married Lovers*. New York: Warner Books, 1986.

Winch, R. *Mate Selection*. New York: Harper, 1958.

Zilbergeld, B., and C. R. Ellison. "Desire Discrepancies and Arousal Problems in Sex Therapy." In S. Leiblum and L. Pervin, eds., *Principles and Practice of Sex Therapy*. New York: Guilford Press, 1980.

Zilbergeld, B., and P. Kilmann. "The Scope and Effectiveness of Sex Therapy." *Psychotherapy* 21 (1984): 319–26.

Index

About the Author

RICHARD DRISCOLL, Ph.D., is a clinical psychologist specializing in marriage and family therapy. He is in independent practice with his wife, who is also a psychologist, and they have three children. His first book is on guidelines for ordinary language psychotherapy.